W9-BYK-167

SINGER

SEWING REFERENCE LIBRARY®

Upholstery Basics

CREATIVE
PUBLISHING
international

MINNETONKA, MINNESOTA

SINGER

SEWING REFERENCE LIBRARY®

Upholstery
Basics

Contents

CREATIVE PUBLISHING international

President: Iain Macfarlane

Library of Congress Cataloging-in-Publication Data
Upholstery basics.
    p. cm. -- (Singer sewing reference library)
  Includes index.
  ISBN 0-86573-318-X (hardcover). -- ISBN 0-86573-319-8 (softcover)
  1. Upholstery. 2. Upholstered furniture. I. Creative Publishing international.
II. Series.
TT198.U573 1997
684.1'2--dc21   97-14879

Books available in this series:
Sewing Essentials, Sewing for the Home, Clothing Care & Repair, Sewing for Style, Sewing Specialty Fabrics, Sewing Activewear, The Perfect Fit, Timesaving Sewing, More Sewing for the Home, Tailoring, Sewing for Children, 101 Sewing Secrets, Sewing Pants That Fit, Quilting by Machine, Decorative Machine Stitching, Creative Sewing Ideas, Sewing Lingerie, Sewing Projects for the Home, Sewing with Knits, More Creative Sewing Ideas, Quilt Projects by Machine, Creating Fashion Accessories, Quick & Easy Sewing Projects, Sewing for Special Occasions, Sewing for the Holidays, Quick & Easy Decorating Projects, Quilted Projects & Garments, Embellished Quilted Projects, Window Treatments, Holiday Projects, Halloween Costumes, Upholstery Basics, Fabric Artistry, The New Sewing with a Serger

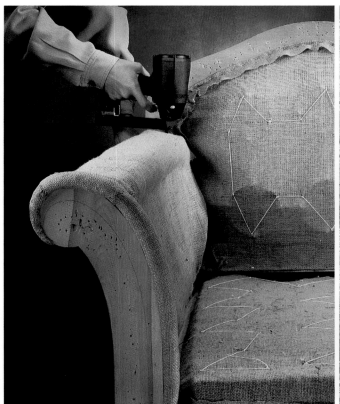

UPHOLSTERY BASICS

Created by: The Editors of Creative
Publishing international, Inc., in
cooperation with the Sewing Education
Department, Singer Sewing Company.
Singer is a trademark of The Singer
Company Limited and is used
under license.

Creative Director: Lisa Rosenthal
Senior Managing Editor: Elaine Perry
Project Manager: Amy Friebe
Writer/Researcher: Linda Neubauer
Senior Art Director: Delores Swanson
Editor: Janice Cauley
Project & Prop Stylists: Coralie Sathre,
  Joanne Wawra
Lead Samplemaker: Phyllis Galbraith
Sewing Staff: Arlene Dohrman,

Phyllis Galbraith, Bridget Haugh,
Kristi Kuhnau, Carol Pilot,
Michelle Skudlarek, Nancy Sundeen
Senior Technical Photo Stylist:
  Bridget Haugh
Technical Photo Stylist: Nancy Sundeen
V. P. Photography & Production: Jim Bindas
Studio Services Manager: Marcia Chambers
Photo Services Coordinator: Cheryl Neisen
Photographers: Kim Bailey, Doug Deutscher,
  Paul Englund, Rex Irmen, Paul Najlis,
  Chuck Nields, Joel Schnell, Steve Smith,
  Greg Wallace, Mark Williams
Publishing Production Manager: Kim Gerber
Desktop Publishing Specialist:
  Laurie Kristensen
Production Staff: Laura Hokkanen,
  Curt Ellering, Michelle Peterson,
  Mike Schauer, Jon Simpson, Kay Wethern
Consultant: Steve Cone

Contributors: A-1 Foam Specialties Co., Inc.;
  Do-It-Yourself Upholstery Supply; New
  York Fabrics, Inc.; Rochford Supply, Inc.

Product information listed on page 127.

Printed on American paper by:
  R. R. Donnelley & Sons Co.
10 9 8 7 6 5 4 3 2

Introduction

Upholstery is often a self-taught craft, learned by experimenting. With this approach, the only instructions for reupholstering a piece of furniture are developed while taking it apart. The obvious dilemma is that you must rely on the cleverness of the person who upholstered before you and risk repeating poor decisions. *Upholstery Basics* is designed to take the guesswork out of the upholstery process. Used as a guide, this book will help you recognize and repeat quality techniques, while avoiding unprofessional, and sometimes costly, errors.

Upholstery, when done well, can be very rewarding. Consider the creative satisfaction of returning a tattered cast-off to its like-new state, as well as the money saved because you didn't have to buy new. The comfort of a favorite chair need not be sacrificed simply because it no longer suits the color scheme of the room. Family heirlooms become more than cherished souvenirs when they are upholstered to blend with the decor of the home.

In the Getting Started section, acquaint yourself with the supplies, tools, and terms used for upholstery. Throughout this section, you will find detailed instructions for some

6

of the most frequently required elements in the upholstery process. Use this section as a reference for completing such tasks as stripping, webbing, tying springs, making cushions, and sewing skirts.

Whether your intent is to tackle one project or begin an ongoing hobby, set up a work space away from the general living area of your home. Depending on the amount of time you have available, projects can take several work sessions to complete. You will want to leave your project, supplies, and tools undisturbed between sessions.

The various furniture pieces in the Upholstery Projects section incorporate a full range of basic upholstery techniques for beginner to intermediate skill levels. Acknowledging the endless furniture design differences, it is likely that you may have to combine techniques from several projects to complete your particular piece. The process for upholstering an easy chair, for example, might include some methods used in both the overstuffed chair and the wing chair. Likewise, an antique carved-wood footstool may feature an attached knife-edge cushion. Compare the design features of your furniture item with those shown, and use the upholstery methods that suit your particular project.

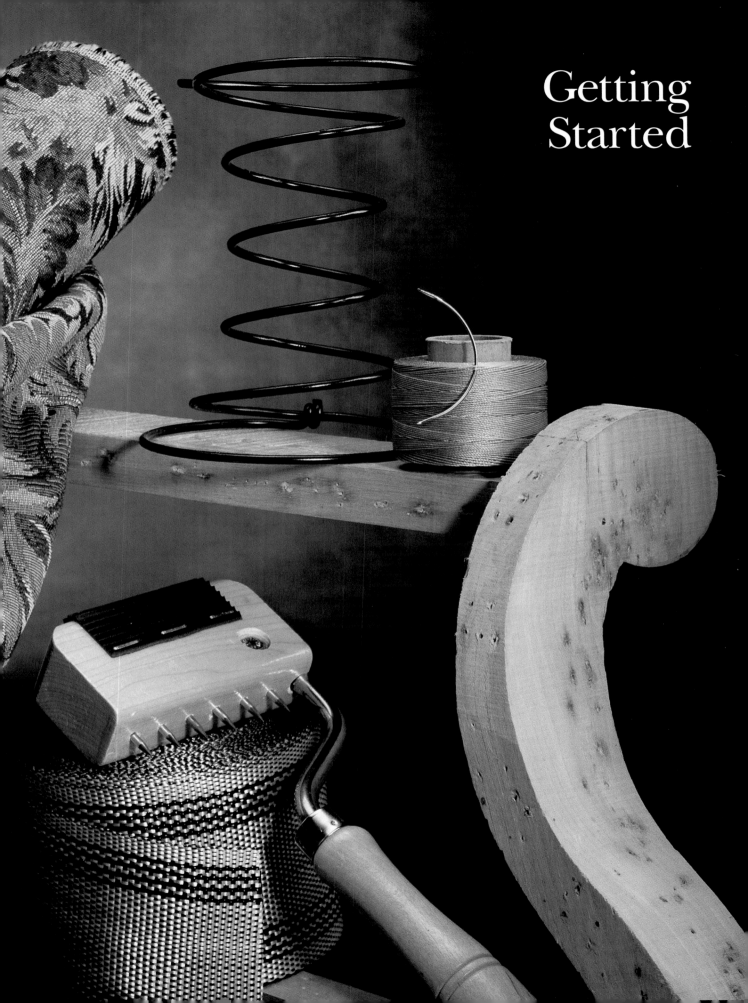

Getting
Started

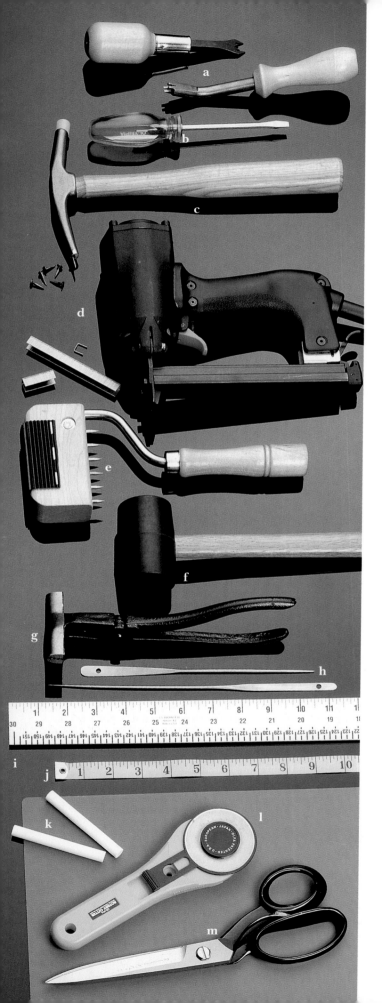

Tools

Quality upholstery cannot be achieved without the use of a few specially designed tools. If you make the initial investment in these tools and learn the proper way to use them, upholstery projects will be easier to complete and produce more satisfactory results. Tools can be purchased at upholstery supply stores or through mail-order catalogs. Check the Yellow Pages for the nearest supplier, or contact the sources listed on page 127.

Stripping & Upholstering Tools

Claw-shaped tack and staple removers (**a**) are designed for removing old tacks and staples when stripping furniture to be reupholstered. A small screwdriver or chisel (**b**) can also be used to remove old tacks or staples. An upholsterer's tack hammer (**c**) has one magnetized tip, so that the hammer holds the tack, leaving your other hand free to hold the fabric. The style shown has a nylon tip, used for inserting decorative tacks. Electric staple gun (**d**) is a fast, efficient way to secure new fabric. Purchase a style that will accommodate both ⅜" (1 cm) and ½" (1.3 cm) staples. Replacing worn or loose webbing is a chore made infinitely easier by using a webbing stretcher (**e**). It works as a lever, allowing you to pull the webbing taut with one hand while tacking or stapling it with the other hand. Mallets (**f**), made of rubber or rawhide, are used to close flexible metal tack strips and to adjust padded surfaces. Stretching pliers (**g**), made for webbing and leather, can also be used to grasp and stretch fabric for stapling to the frame. Upholstery regulators (**h**), available in 8" (20.5 cm) and 10" (25.5 cm) lengths, are long metal skewers with multiple uses. The flattened end of the regulator is used for pleating or forcing padding into tight corners. The sharp end of the regulator is used to make a hole in the fabric by gently separating yarns in the weave. Once the padding has been moved, the hole can be closed by gently coaxing the yarns back into position.

Measuring, Marking & Cutting Tools

Frequently, during the upholstery process, a yardstick (meter stick) (**i**) is necessary. Since most upholstery is not flat, you will also need a good-quality cloth tape measure (**j**). Dustless white chalk sticks (**k**) are used for marking out cutting lines on the fabric, for tailoring cushion patterns, and for various other marking tasks. A cutting mat and rotary cutter (**l**) make short work of cutting fabric strips for welting. Also be sure to have heavy-duty shears (**m**) for cutting the upholstery fabrics, battings, and other supplies.

Pins & Needles

There are several hand sewing needles designed for upholstery work. Curved needles (a) are used for blindstitching fabric in places where stapling or tacking are not possible. They are also used to secure springs to webbing and burlap. Round-point curved needles are used for fabrics, while flat-point needles are used for leather or vinyl. Button needles (b), available in a variety of lengths from 6" to 18" (15 to 46 cm), are used to secure buttons to upholstered furniture and to stitch through padding to secure it to a foundation. Upholstery pins (c) are used to hold fabric in place temporarily before tacking or sewing.

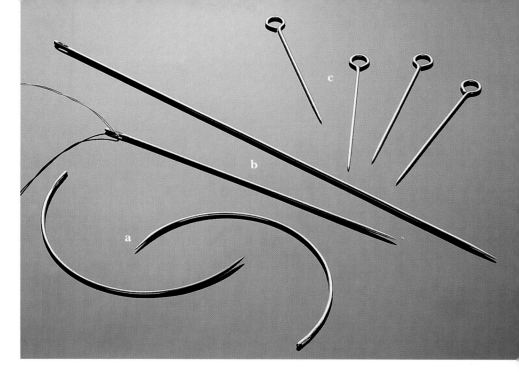

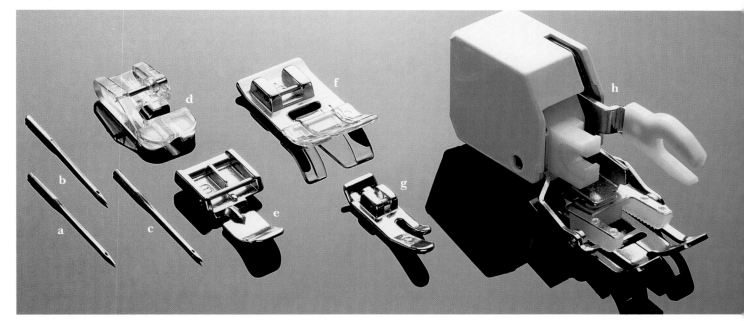

Sewing Machine Equipment

Though professional upholsterers use industrial sewing machines, most home sewing machines can successfully handle lightweight to mediumweight upholstery fabrics. Some specially designed accessories can help to make the job easier.

Insert heavy-duty needles into the sewing machine. For lightweight to mediumweight upholstery fabrics, use size 16/100 (a); for heavyweight fabrics use size 18/110 (b). Specially designed needles for sewing on leathers and vinyls (c) have a wedge-shaped point that cuts a tiny slit, rather than a round hole.

A welting foot is very helpful for sewing continuous welting without puckers. A deep groove cut in the bottom of the foot rides over the fabric-covered cord, feeding the layers of fabric evenly for a smooth, tight fit. If a welting foot is not available for your sewing machine brand, you may be able to use a generic foot, such as the Pearls 'N Piping Foot™ (d) made by Creative Feet, which is designed to accommodate welting and trim up to ¼" (6 mm) thick. A zipper foot (e) is essential for inserting zippers into cushions and can also be used for making welting, if a welting foot is not available. A general-purpose foot (f) or a straight-stitch foot (g) can be used for sewing any seam that does not have welting. An Even Feed® foot (h) can be used to keep layers from shifting when sewing unwelted seams in difficult fabrics, such as upholstery velvet.

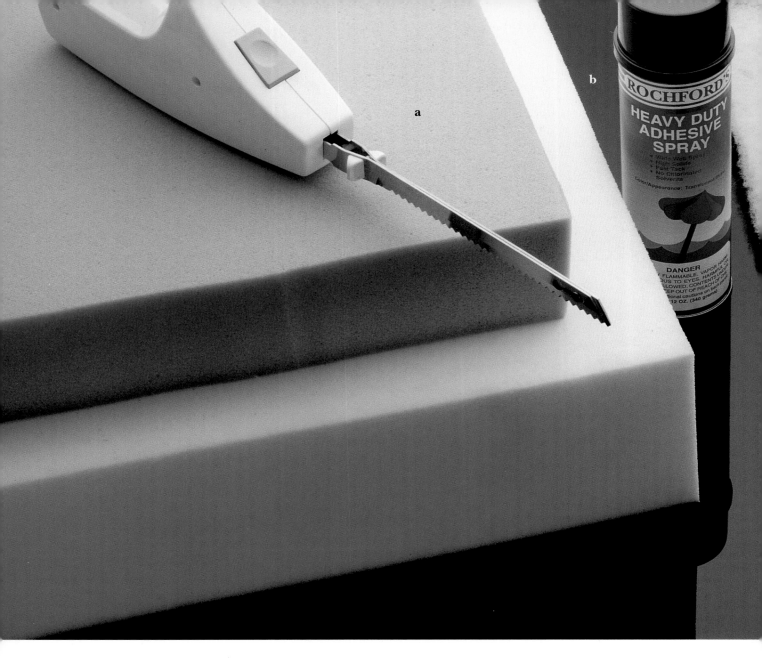

Upholstery Supplies

The basic shape and foundation padding in any piece of furniture is formed using a variety of materials. Many modern pieces use synthetic foam to provide the basic shaping and are padded with polyester batting. Others, especially older pieces, are shaped and padded using natural-fiber foundation materials, such as rubberized hair or coirtex, and then padded with cotton batting. Often, furniture contains both natural and synthetic foundation materials, as when an overstuffed chair has natural-fiber padding in the arms and back, and a foam seat cushion wrapped with polyester batting.

When reupholstering a piece of furniture that was originally padded with natural-fiber materials, reuse the materials intact, if the foundation is still in very good shape. Supplement or replace the padding with either cotton or polyester batting. If the original foundation materials are not reusable, build a new foundation using foam and polyester batting, which are more readily available, more economical, and easier to work with.

To retain authenticity, reupholster antiques using natural materials. In stripping older furniture, it is common to discover padding materials such as curled hair, moss, tow, and straw. If desired, these materials can be reused, though it may be impossible to supplement the padding with more of the same material, and working with these materials requires more time and expertise. Often some additional cotton batting is all that is needed to restore the piece to its original shape and firmness.

Padding Materials

Foam (**a**) can be purchased in many thicknesses and degrees of firmness. High-resiliency foams are used for seat cushions because of their superior ability to retain their shape. Upholsterers cut foam with an electric foam saw that features a vertical blade. An electric kitchen knife can also be used, but care must be taken to keep the blade perpendicular to the surface of the foam for perfectly squared cuts. Foam that is 1" (2.5 cm) thick or thinner can be cut with shears. Spray foam adhesive (**b**) is used to secure foam to webbing or polyester batting.

Bonded polyester batting (**c**), noted for its loft and resiliency, is commonly used in most modern uphol-stered furniture. Polyester batting is cut with shears. It can be stapled directly to framework and need not be covered by an inner cover.

Cotton batting (**d**) is available in different grades of purity, depending on the intended use. Economy grades of cotton tend to be less fluffy and may contain seeds and other impurities. For surface padding, a high grade of cotton is used. Cotton batting is gently torn to size, rather than cut.

Coirtex (**e**) is a stiff brown padding material made from coconut fiber. Because it is rather thin, it is suitable for areas that require minimal foundation padding, such as chair decks or thinly padded chair backs or arms.

Rubberized hair (**f**) is used when a thicker or fuller appearance is required. Because it tends to make a crunching sound when it is compressed, it should not be used in seat areas.

Foundation Fabrics

Cambric (**a**) is a black fabric used to cover the bottom of a furniture piece for a finished look and to act as a dustcover.

Burlap (**b**) is used as a covering over springs or webbing to form the support base.

Denim (**c**) is a strong, thin fabric, available in many colors to coordinate with upholstery fabric. It is used to cover the deck area of the chair and to line skirts.

Webbing, purchased in rolls, is available in both synthetic (**d**) and jute (**e**) forms. Synthetic webbing is stronger than true jute webbing and does not rot over time or due to moisture. Jute webbing, however, is necessary for reupholstering antiques to retain their authenticity.

An edge roll (**f**) is a long, firmly stuffed tube that is attached over a wood or wire edge to cushion it. Edge rolls, available in a variety of sizes, keep padding from shifting, while reducing wear on the outer fabric.

Threads, Twines & Cords

Polyester thread (**g**) is the best choice for upholstery sewing using the conventional sewing machine. It offers strength, without being too thick. Nylon thread, size #18 (**h**), works well for any hand sewing that must be done, because it fits the eyes of curved needles and is available in many colors. Nylon button twine (**i**) is a strong twine used for various tasks, such as fastening buttons, hand-stitching edge rolls and nosing seams, and securing springs to webbing and burlap. Spring twine (**j**), available in both jute and polyester, is used for tying springs (page 32). Welt cording (**k**) is most commonly used in the 5/32" (3.8 mm) size. Cotton cording provides the best results for most upholstery fabrics.

Nails, Tacks, Staples & Zippers

Webbing nails (**a**), as the name implies, are used to secure webbing to the frame. Because they are narrow and have sharp points, they can hold the webbing securely without damaging the wood. They are also used to secure the tails of hand-sewing threads, and in other cases where upholstery tacks are not sufficient. The most commonly used sizes of upholstery tacks (**b**) are #3 and #6, the smaller number relating to the shorter tacks. Upholstery tacks are packaged in sterile condition, recognizing that the most convenient place to hold them is in the mouth. Staples (**c**) are the fastener of choice for most upholstery tasks, except reupholstering antique furniture, in which case, tacks are used. Decorative tacks (**d**) come in many sizes, designs, and finishes to complement any fabric or furniture style. Tack strip (**e**) is card-board stripping, ½" (1.3 cm) wide, used to maintain a straight, sharp line between upholstered fabric pieces. Tacking strip (**f**) has tacks spaced evenly apart for securing fabric panels invisibly, when tacking is not possible. Flexible metal tacking strip (**g**) is used for the same purpose in curved areas.

Strong zippers, available with either metal or nylon teeth, are used for cushion cover closures. They can be purchased in predetermined lengths (**h**) or as continuous zipper tape (**i**), which can be cut to size and fitted with a zipper pull.

Upholstery Fabrics

The fabric selected for the upholstery project has a great impact on the final appearance, comfort, and durability of the furniture piece. Color and design obviously play a large part in the decision making, but it is also important to consider the fiber content, weave structure, and any surface treatment applied to the fabric.

Various fibers are used in upholstery fabrics, including natural and synthetic types. Some natural fibers come from a plant source, such as cotton, linen, or ramie. Others are animal products, such as wool or silk. Synthetic fibers include nylon, acrylic, polyester, and olefin. Rayon is a man-made fiber, produced from a plant source.

Each fiber has characteristics that make it desirable in some ways, though limiting its appeal in other ways. Often fibers are blended in a fabric to capitalize on the strengths of each, while minimizing their weaknesses. Rayon, for example, does not wear well but is often blended with fibers that are stronger, because it accepts dye well and gives the fabric luster. Natural fibers are generally easier to work with than synthetics. However, synthetics blended with natural fibers often produce a more stable fabric.

Some fabrics are woven so the pattern or design is *railroaded*. This means running the lengthwise grain horizontally on the piece of furniture rather than in the normal vertical direction. Railroading can save a considerable amount of yardage, especially on sofas.

Fabrics can be grouped into categories according to their weave or surface design. Plain weaves (a) are the simplest of weaves. Their durability depends on the strength of the yarns and closeness of the weave. Satin weaves (b) are woven so that yarns float on the surface, giving the fabric a subtle sheen. They are often printed and can be used for drapery or upholstery. Rib weaves (c) are a variation of the plain weave. Finer yarns alternate with heavier yarns, giving the ribbed effect. Their durability is limited because the yarns are exposed to friction during use. Pile weaves (d) have cut or uncut loops that stand up on the surface of the fabric. Velvets and chenilles are pile weaves. Jacquard weaves (e) have a woven-in design, created on a special loom. Damasks, tapestries, and brocades are all jaquard weaves. Novelty weaves (f) are created by using a variation or a combination of the basic weaves.

Most upholstery fabrics are treated with a stain-resistant or crease-resistant finish, greatly increasing the durability of the fabric. A latex finish is sometimes applied to the back of loosely woven or pile fabrics to keep the grainline from shifting or to hold the pile in place. A heavy latex backing makes the fabric quite stiff and difficult to sew.

Furniture Parts

Learning the process and techniques of furniture upholstery will be eased by knowing the correct names of the furniture parts, both in their upholstered state and stripped to the bare frame. Use the labeled photographs below and opposite to become familiar with these part names. Depending on the project, the furniture piece you are upholstering may not have all the parts that are shown on the chair below. Or it may have parts not shown, such as a skirt, arm boxing, or back boxing.

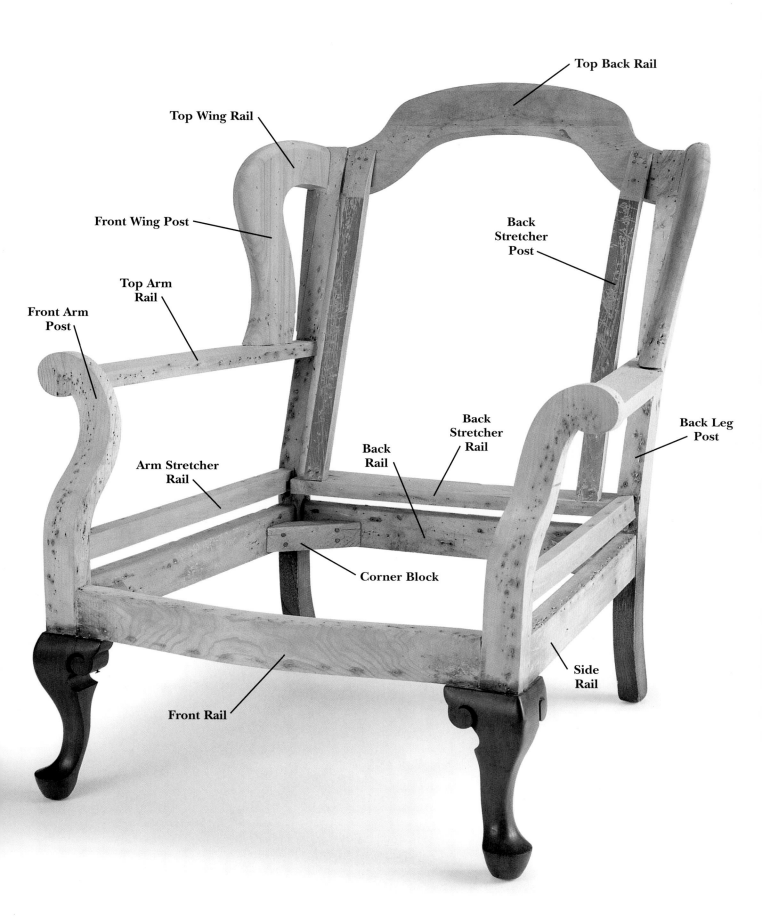

Top Back Rail

Top Wing Rail

Front Wing Post

Back Stretcher Post

Top Arm Rail

Front Arm Post

Back Stretcher Rail

Back Rail

Back Leg Post

Arm Stretcher Rail

Corner Block

Side Rail

Front Rail

Measure and record the actual size of each section, including the approximate amount of hidden fabric. Determine the cut size of each section by adding the necessary allowances for pulling and stapling or for seams, as explained at right. Double-check your list to be sure that you have not forgotten any sections. Then diagram the fabric layout from the determined cut sizes.

Measuring & Cutting

Before stripping the cover from the furniture, take careful measurements of every piece. This is important not only for determining yardage requirements, but also for planning an efficient cutting layout. Keep in mind that most pieces will be cut out as rectangles and trimmed to shape as they are attached to the furniture. It is important, therefore, to measure each piece at its longest and widest points.

Make a list of all the pieces that will be needed, and record the measurements as they are taken. Write the measurements as *length* times *width*, remembering that length is always the up-and-down measurement; width is always the side-to-side measurement. Then add in the necessary allowances, adding a 2" (5 cm) pulling allowance to each edge that will be attached by stapling or tacking and ½" (1.3 cm) seam allowances to pieces that are sewn together. Finally, measure the total length of all the welting used in the furniture piece. The example chart below was developed from the measurements of the chair shown opposite. Your measurement chart may include pieces not listed on the example chart, such as a skirt, arm boxing or back boxing.

The total length of some pieces, including inside back, inside arms, and inside wings, includes fabric that cannot be seen before stripping. From the point where the inside back meets the deck, for example, hidden fabric extends down several inches (centimeters) and is attached to the back rail of the chair. Include the approximate amount of hidden fabric in your actual measurements.

To avoid wasting expensive upholstery fabric, strips of inexpensive fabrics or used upholstery fabrics, called *stretchers,* are often sewn to the pieces in hidden locations. To determine the cut size of a piece that will get a stretcher, measure the *visible* fabric and add ½" (1.3 cm) for each edge that is attached to another piece by a seam and 2" (5 cm) to each edge that will have a stretcher. This will ensure that the stretcher is not visible in the finished upholstery. Cut the stretcher to the size of the *hidden* fabric plus 2" (5 cm).

After measuring, diagram the layout of all the pieces on graph paper, as in the examples on pages 22 and 23. Fabric yardage can be accurately determined from the diagram. To avoid costly mistakes, purchase fabric only after completing the measuring and layout diagram.

Cut the end of the fabric squarely, either by following a thread in the weave, using a carpenter's square, or by aligning a straightedge to the pattern repeat markings on the selvages. Transfer the diagram to the right side of the fabric, marking out the cutting lines with chalk and measuring from the squared end. Label the wrong side of every piece with its location as it is cut. Also, draw a chalk line near the lower edge to indicate the downward direction.

Measurement Chart Example

Piece	Actual Size (includes hidden fabric)		Allowances ½" (1.3 cm) seam 2" (5 cm) pulling		Cut Size
Front Band (FB)	5½" × 21" (14 × 53.5 cm)	+	2½" × 4" (6.5 × 10 cm)	=	8" × 25" (20.5 × 63.5 cm)
Nosing (N)	6" × 21" (15 × 53.5 cm)	+	1" × 4" (2.5 × 10 cm)	=	7" × 25" (18 × 63.5 cm)
Inside Back (IB)	36" × 32" (91.5 × 81.5 cm)	+	4" × 4" (10 × 10 cm)	=	40" × 36" (102 × 91.5 cm)
Inside Arm (IA)	27" × 27" (68.5 × 68.5 cm)	+	4" × 4" (10 × 10 cm)	=	31" × 31" (78.5 × 78.5 cm)
Front Arm Band (FAB)	18" × 8" (46 × 20.5 cm)	+	4" × 2½" (10 × 6.5 cm)	=	22" × 10½" (56 × 26.8 cm)
Inside Wing (IW)	17" × 9" (43 × 23 cm)	+	4" × 4" (10 × 10 cm)	=	21" × 13" (53.5 × 33 cm)
Outside Arm (OA)	14" × 26" (35.5 × 66 cm)	+	4" × 4" (10 × 10 cm)	=	18" × 30" (46 × 76 cm)
Outside Wing (OW)	15" × 7" (38 × 18 cm)	+	4" × 4" (10 × 10 cm)	=	19" × 11" (48.5 × 28 cm)
Outside Back (OB)	30" × 23" (76 × 58.5 cm)	+	4" × 4" (10 × 10 cm)	=	34" × 27" (86.5 × 68.5 cm)
Arm Panel (AP)	15½" × 4" (39.3 × 10 cm)	+	4" × 4" (10 × 10 cm)	=	19½" × 8" (49.8 × 20.5 cm)
Cushion* (C)	22" × 19" (56 × 48.5 cm)				
Cushion Boxing* (CB)	4" × 63" (10 × 160 cm)				
Zipper Boxing* (ZB)	2" × 26" (5 × 66 cm)				
Welting** (W)	251" (637.5 cm)				266" × 1⅝" (676 × 4 cm)

*The cut size of cushion pieces, cushion boxing, and zipper boxing are determined after tailoring a pattern for the cushion (page 50).

**Additional welting length is allowed for seaming and waste.

Fabric Layout Diagrams

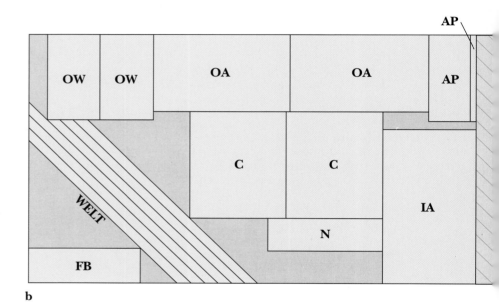

a

Layout for Fabric without a Pattern. (a) Most upholstery fabrics are 54" (137 cm) wide. Because the pieces are cut as rectangles, this layout is suitable for fabric with or without a nap.

Layout for Railroaded Fabric. (b) If the fabric can be railroaded (page 17), lay out the pieces so that their length runs on the crosswise grain. This is often a more efficient layout.

b

Layout for Patterned Fabric. (c) Special consideration must be given to the length of the repeat and the pattern arrangement. Large motifs, indicated by dots on the diagram, are centered on the exposed areas of prominent pieces, such as cushion tops and bottoms, inside and outside backs, and inside and outside arms. The pattern should flow uninterrupted from the top of the inside back to the bottom of the front band or skirt, aligning horizontally, as well.

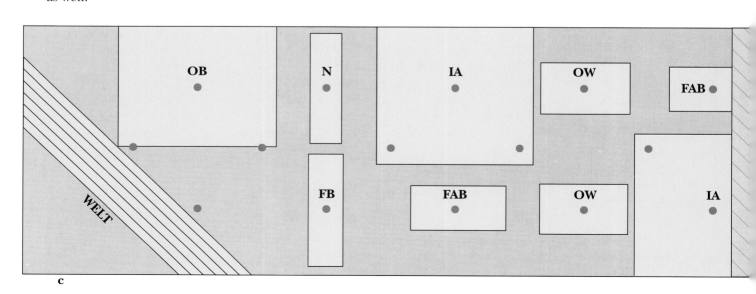

c

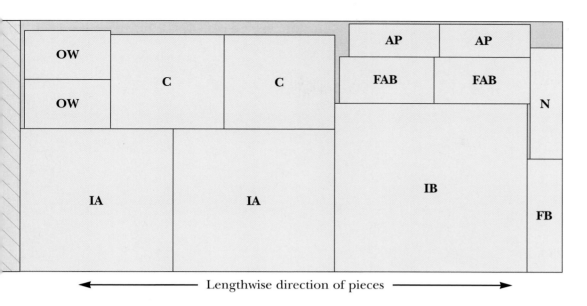

Lengthwise direction of pieces

AP Continued

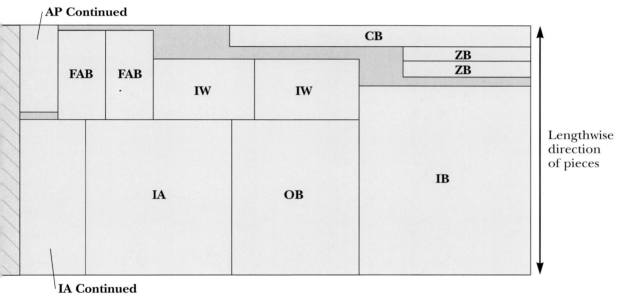

Lengthwise
direction
of pieces

IA Continued

FA Continued   CB   ZB   ← Lengthwise direction of pieces →

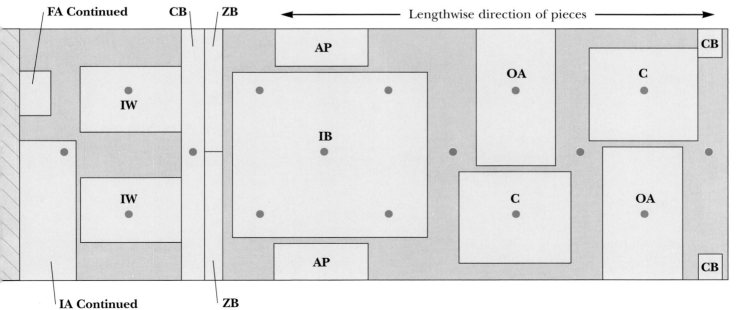

IA Continued   ZB

Cover work area with tarp. Stripping upholstery is messy and dusty. Discard used tacks, nails, staples, tack strips, and tacking strips; they are not reusable. Discard any musty-smelling foundation materials. Take detailed notes, and draw sketches or take pictures with every piece that is removed. These will become your reupholstery instructions.

Stripping Furniture

Removing the old cover from a furniture piece is an educational experience, so take notes. Before removing even one staple, sketch or take pictures of any unique details you wish to reproduce in the new cover, such as the pleating arrangement on an arm front or a series of tucks at a nosing corner. Determine any areas that need more padding. Label each fabric piece with its location and direction. List the seams and joints that have welting, and measure the total length of welting used. Once removed, the fabric pieces are merely puzzling flat shapes.

Avoid back strain and sore knees by standing the project on a raised platform or padded sawhorses. You can then do the upholstery work while standing or sitting at a comfortable height, without repeatedly bending over or kneeling.

Loosen or remove pieces in the reverse order from that in which they were attached to the frame. For example, if reupholstering a wing chair, first remove the skirt, dustcover, and any welting around the lower edge. Then remove the outside back, outside arms, and outside wings. Loosen the inside back, inside arms, and inside wings, leaving them staple-basted (page 68) in position to keep the padding in place. Remove the deck and nosing last. As each piece is loosened or removed, record the method used to attach it to adjoining pieces or to the frame: machine-sewn, hand-sewn, stapled, or attached with a tacking strip. Set the pieces aside for reference throughout the upholstery project.

Strip the padding and foundation only as far as necessary. Check to see if the frame is sturdy, if the webbing and springs are secure, and if the padding needs to be replaced or replenished. Some furniture will have a muslin cover just under the outer cover. This can be left intact if only the outer cover needs to be replaced. However, if you encounter any additional layers of old upholstery fabric, remove them.

Tips for Stripping Upholstery

Removing tacks, nails, and staples. 1) Hold the tack lifter or staple remover at sharp angle, with tip touching the wood at edge of tack, nail, or staple. Strike end of handle with side of tack hammer, wedging tip under tack, nail, or staple.

2) Pry tack, nail, or staple up from the wood.

3) Grasp tack, nail, or staple with pliers; roll pliers in direction of wood grain, extracting tack, nail, or staple. (Extracting against the wood grain damages and weakens wood.) Remove *all* tacks, nails, and staples. Pound in any broken points that cannot be removed.

Easy Frame Repairs

Because you are about to spend considerable time, energy, and money on reupholstering, it is important to begin with a structurally sound furniture frame. After removing the outer cover, check to see if there are any loose joints or cracked rails or posts. Minor repair work can be done with minimal carpentry skills.

This is also the opportune time to completely refinish any exposed wood, if necessary. However, shallow scratches and general dullness can be corrected with simpler techniques.

Repair minor scratches, using touch-up markers in the same color as the stained and finished woodwork.

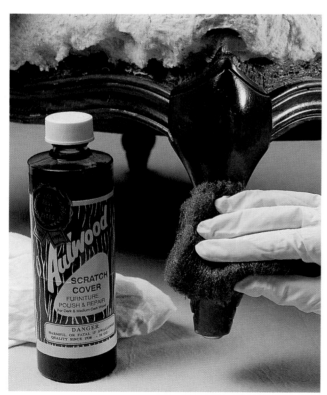

Clean dull finish, using wood polish and cleaner and gently rubbing with extra-fine steel wool. Cleaners containing lemon oil are especially beneficial.

Tighten loose corner blocks by first applying wood glue and then inserting wood screws.

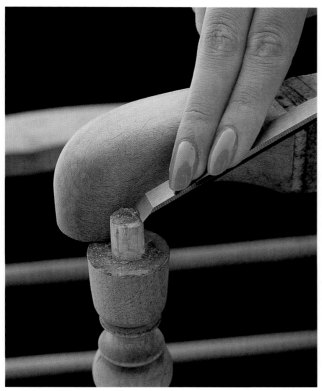

To reglue loose joints. 1) Open joint. Apply hot vinegar to old glue to soften; scrape away old glue.

2) Apply ample amount of wood glue to joint. Close joint; clamp tightly. Allow to dry, following glue manufacturer's directions.

Cracked rail or post. 1) Inject wood glue into crack, using glue syringe.

2) Clamp rail or post securely. Allow to dry, following glue manufacturer's directions.

Webbing

The support base for most furniture consists of inter-woven strips of webbing. Webbing is used in seats, backs, and arms as a base for springs or padding, and ultimately takes the weight of the person sitting or leaning on it. Whenever reupholstering a piece of furniture, check the existing webbing for wear and tautness. Unless the furniture is fairly new, it is probably worth the time and effort to replace the webbing with new taut strips.

Webbing is usually 3½" (9 cm) wide and available in several strengths. Synthetic webbing and webbing made from a blend of jute and synthetic fibers, such as Jutelac™, are very stable and can be used in all locations. Jute webbing with a red stripe is designed to be used in seats, because it will not stretch. Jute webbing with a black stripe is slightly less stable, and is used for the arms and backs of chairs and sofas. A webbing stretcher (page 10) makes the job much easier, and is essential for attaching the strips with the proper tautness. For efficiency and easy handling, work from the roll of webbing; do not precut webbing strips. Webbing nails must be used for securing seat and back webbing. Webbing on parts that do not bear much weight may be secured with staples, if desired.

Generally, a seat with springs is webbed on the underside of the frame; a seat without springs is webbed on the upper side of the frame. Arms, backs, and wings without springs are webbed on the inner surfaces; backs or arms with springs are webbed on the outer surfaces. The more weight the webbing must hold, the closer together the strips should be, always allowing at least ¼" (6 mm) between them to prevent abrasion. Webbing on arms or wings that will not bear weight can be spaced up to 4" (10 cm) apart.

YOU WILL NEED

Webbing.
Webbing nails; #6 upholstery tacks; tack hammer.
Webbing stretcher.

Synthetic webbing, pulled taut and properly secured, provides a firm, long-lasting support base.

How to Attach Webbing to a Seat

1) Mark centers of front and back rails. Determine number and spacing of strips. Fold back webbing 1" (2.5 cm). Place folded end ¼" (6 mm) from outer edge of back rail, centering strip over center mark if using odd number of strips or placing strip to one side of center mark if using even number. Secure folded end to rail, using five webbing nails arranged as shown (nail heads painted for visibility).

2) Draw webbing across frame opening to front rail, centering strip over center front mark or to one side of center. Place webbing stretcher under webbing, catching webbing securely on stretcher spikes.

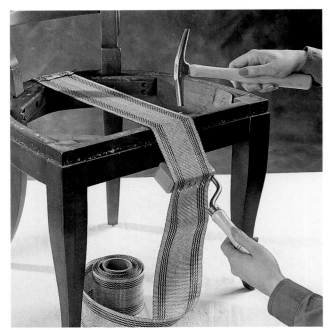

3) Wedge stretcher under front rail. Pull webbing taut, taking care not to bend rails; insert three #6 tacks in center of rail to hold webbing.

4) Trim webbing 1" (2.5 cm) beyond outer edge of rail. Fold back end of strip so fold is ¼" (6 mm) from outer edge of rail. Insert five webbing nails, positioned as shown.

5) Attach remaining webbing strips from back to front, evenly spaced; alternate from side to side of center. Stretch all strips equally taut.

6) Mark centers of side rails. Attach first webbing strip in sideways direction, at or to one side of center; weave strip over and under previously attached strips. Attach remaining strips, alternating from side to side of center and reversing weave pattern of adjacent strips.

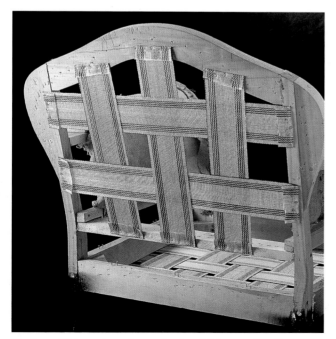

Back webbing. Attach vertical webbing strips first, stretching from bottom to top. Weave and secure horizontal strips, starting near center of back.

Arm or wing webbing. Space webbing strips up to 4" (10 cm) apart, providing minimal foundation for padding. For chair without arm stretcher post, pin back end of front-to-back strip until inside back and inside arm cover pieces have been attached.

Springs

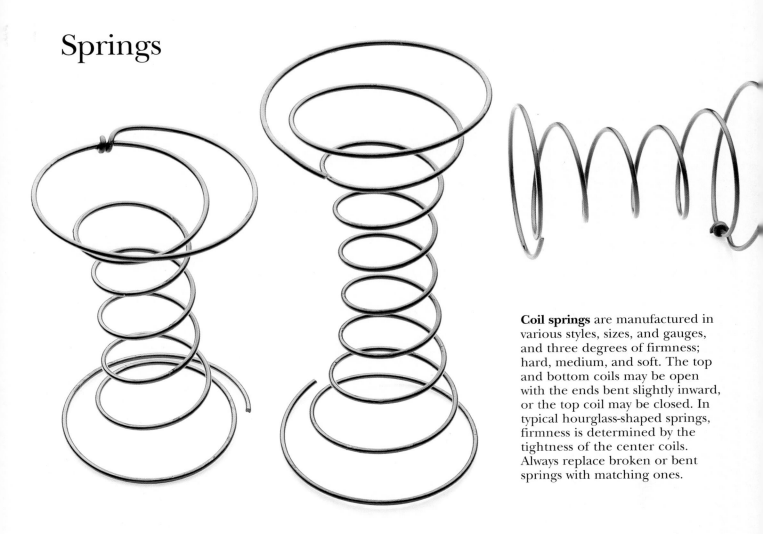

Coil springs are manufactured in various styles, sizes, and gauges, and three degrees of firmness; hard, medium, and soft. The top and bottom coils may be open with the ends bent slightly inward, or the top coil may be closed. In typical hourglass-shaped springs, firmness is determined by the tightness of the center coils. Always replace broken or bent springs with matching ones.

The basic shape and resilience of upholstered furniture is achieved with the use of steel springs. Depending on the style and age of the furniture, it may contain either *coil springs* or *sinuous springs*.

Coil springs are commonly found in seats and may also provide shape in arms and backs. Several coil springs, arranged in rows, are individually sewn to webbing and then systematically tied together, so that they work as a unit. In some furniture, the coil springs are attached to metal crossbars, rather than webbing, and replacement parts may be difficult to find. The entire system can be rebuilt with a webbing base, if necessary. Often, the coil springs are tied or clipped to an edge wire, secured around all or part of the outer edge. This is used for a flat surface, such as the deck of an overstuffed chair. Spring systems for dome-shaped seats, backs, or ottomans are tied without edge wires.

Some modern furniture is constructed with *sinuous springs,* heavy steel wire shaped in repeating S-curves. These are attached with metal clips to the furniture frame and then tied together with spring twine to prevent them from tipping sideways. In stripping a

piece of furniture with sinuous springs, you may find that they are linked to each other by small helical springs or metal straps, rather than spring twine.

Before reupholstering a piece of furniture, you should check the condition of the spring system. If it is intact and sturdy, the piece can be reupholstered as it is. Any broken or bent springs must be replaced, using a spring of the same gauge, size, and degree of firmness. To be assured of buying the correct spring, compare it to one from the system that is still in good condition. It is a good idea to retie the entire spring system if any of the twines have loosened or broken, or if the webbing supporting the springs needs to be replaced.

In the spring-tying methods described on pages 34 to 43, the springs in each row are lashed together with the first twine, making simple loops over the coils. This enables you to set the height of the springs and adjust their positions before permanently tying them with the second twine. Tying springs may seem complicated, but if you follow this method and use the recommended knots, the system will remain secure and well shaped for many years.

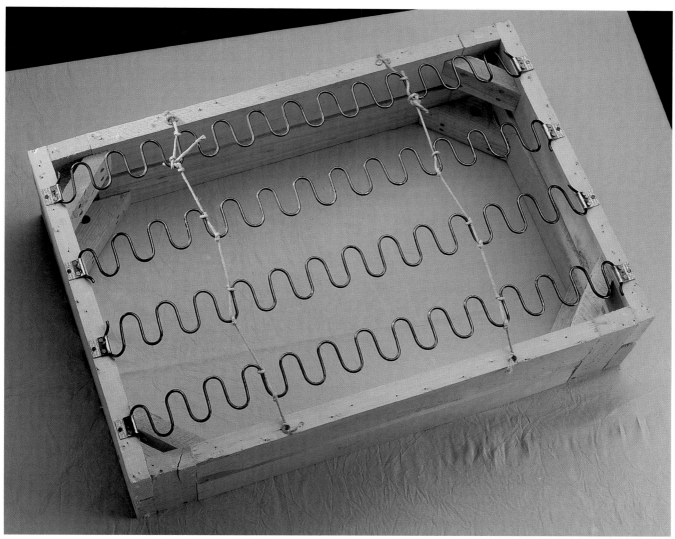

Sinuous springs are used in furniture when a low profile is desired. Once attached to the frame, they should rise in a slight arc, no more than 1½" (3.8 cm) high. Because they are very durable, sinuous springs rarely need to be replaced but may need to be retied, using clove hitch knots or overhand knots.

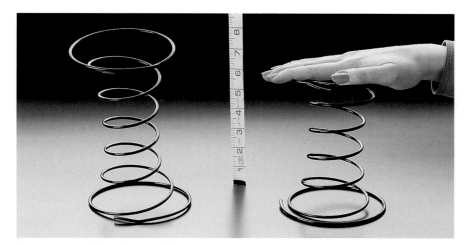

Compress coil spring until it resists compression, to determine the height at which it should be tied. Seat springs are typically compresssed 1½" (3.8 cm) below their actual height.

YOU WILL NEED

Coil spring systems:

Coil springs; purchase replacements of same gauge, size, and firmness as originals.

6" curved needle, nylon button twine, for stitching coil springs to webbing.

Spring twine.

Webbing nails.

Ruler.

Edge wire, for edge wire system.

Sinuous spring system:

Sinuous springs, clips, nails; purchase replacements of same length and gauge as originals.

Spring twine.

Knots Used to Tie Springs

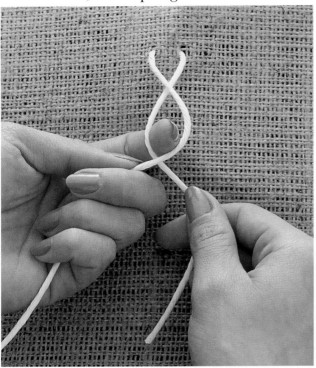

Slipknot. 1) Take one stitch, leaving a tail. Hold long end of twine in left hand, tail in right. Hook tail with index finger of left hand, pulling the tail behind other twine.

2) Turn left hand over, twisting twines.

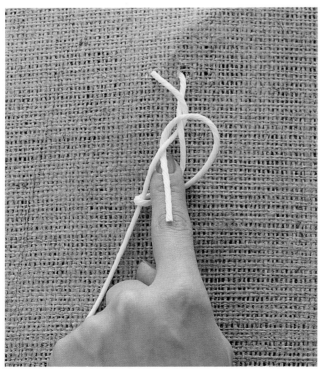

3) Wrap tail over twisted twines above index finger, wrapping to back of twist; insert tail end in first loop above finger.

4) Remove index finger; pull on long end of twine to tighten.

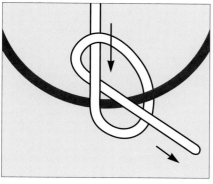

Overhand knot.

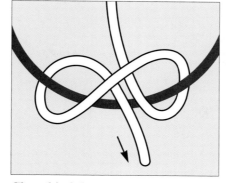

Clove hitch knot.

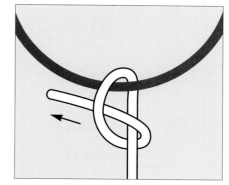

Half hitch knot.

How to Sew Coil Springs to Webbing

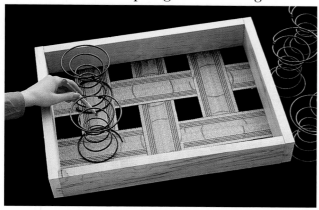

1) Arrange springs over webbing in desired row formation, placing springs over webbing intersections, 2" to 4" (5 to 10 cm) apart; follow original arrangement, if possible. Mark locations with chalk. (Marker was used here for visibility.) If using open-ended springs, position so top open ends of springs in back row face forward; remaining open ends face backward.

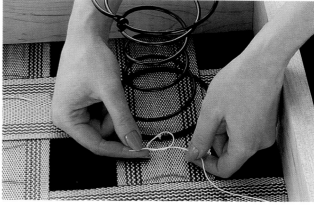

2) Thread 6" (15 cm) curved needle with nylon button twine. Beginning with a corner spring, insert needle from top of webbing, next to bottom coil. Take one short stitch, coming back through webbing close to opposite side of coil; leave tail for knotting. Secure stitch with slipknot. Tie overhand knot over slipknot.

3) Insert needle back through webbing to underside. Stitch spring to webbing with three more stitches, arranging stitches so that last stitch is located near next spring. Secure each stitch with an overhand knot on underside of webbing.

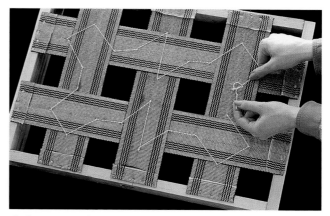

4) Secure each spring with four stitches, working one entire row; proceed to next row. Plan stitch placement so that last stitch on each spring is near first stitch on next spring. Lock all stitches between first and last stitch with overhand knots; lock the last stitch with slipknot, followed by two overhand knots.

How to Tie Springs for a Domed Surface

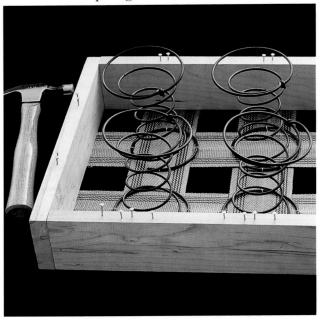

1) **Drive** two webbing nails, spaced ½" (1.3 cm) apart, halfway into rail at center of each row of springs on all rails. On front rail and one side rail, drive two more nails halfway into rail, each spaced 1" (2.5 cm) to outside of center nails.

2) **Cut** spring twine for each row, with length equal to four times the distance between rails. Fold twine in half. Slip folded loop between two nails on back rail; wrap loop back over nails, as shown. Pull twine snugly around nails. Drive nails tightly into rail, securing twine. Repeat for each set of nails on back rail and on one side rail.

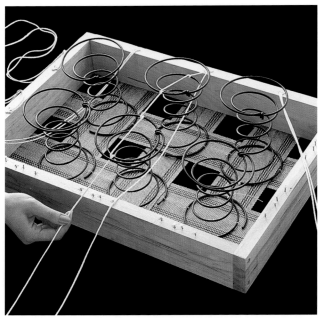

3) **Lash** row of springs together, working from back to front and starting with row at or near center. Follow diagram (**a**), page 42; use single twine, wrapping *over* and around each spring coil in simple loops.

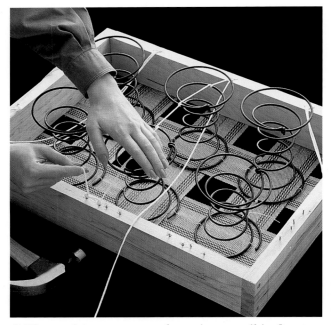

4) **Wrap** twine once around one inner nail in front rail; hold twine taut with one hand while adjusting height and position of springs with other hand. Springs should stand perpendicular to webbing; top coils of front and back springs should angle slightly toward rails. Wrap twine around outer nail; drive nails tightly into rail.

5) Repeat steps 3 and 4 for all rows from back to front, checking height and position of springs frequently.

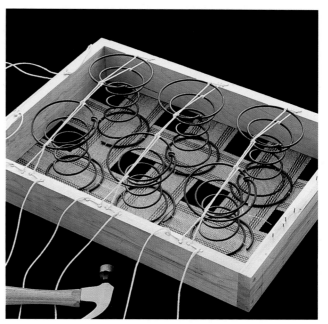

6) Tie spring coils, using remaining twine and following diagram **(b)**, page 42. Use clove hitch knots or overhand knots at each location; tie knots over simple loops that share locations. Keep twine tautness equal to tautness of first twine. Wrap twine around remaining nails; drive nails tightly into rail. Repeat for each back-to-front row.

7) Tie springs in side-to-side rows, following diagram **(a)** for the first twine and diagram **(b)** for the second twine; use clove hitch knots or overhand knots at each location for both twines, tying knots with equal tautness to previously tied twines.

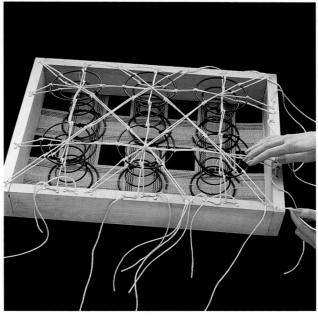

8) Lay straightedge across center of the springs in diagonal row; mark rails at aligned points. Repeat for all diagonal rows. Drive two webbing nails, spaced ½" (1.3 cm) apart, halfway into rail at each mark. Follow step 7 for each diagonal row. Cut tails to about 3" (7.5 cm).

How to Tie Springs with an Edge Wire

1) **Follow** steps 1 and 2 on page 36, omitting nails and twine on front side-to-side row and cutting twine for back-to-front rows six times the distance between rails. Lash row of springs together from back to front, using single twine; start with row at or near center. Follow diagram (c), page 42; wrap *over* and around each spring coil in simple loops.

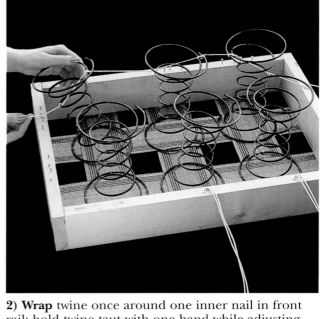

2) **Wrap** twine once around one inner nail in front rail; hold twine taut with one hand while adjusting height and position of springs with other hand. All springs, except front one, should stand perpendicular to webbing. Pull front spring forward until front edge of top coil is even with front edge of rail. Wrap twine around outer nail; drive nails tightly into rail.

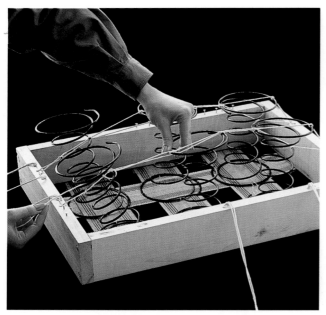

3) **Lash** each back-to-front row, checking height and position of springs frequently. Tie spring coils, using remaining twine and following diagram (d), page 43. Use clove hitch knots or overhand knots at each location; tie knots over simple loops that share locations. Keep twine tautnesss equal to tautness of first twine. Wrap twine around remaining nails; drive nails tightly into rail.

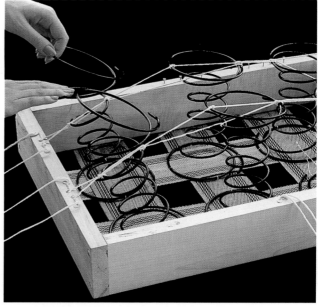

4) **Finish tying** all front-to-back rows. Spread first and second coils of front springs, increasing their resiliency. This is called "breaking" the springs.

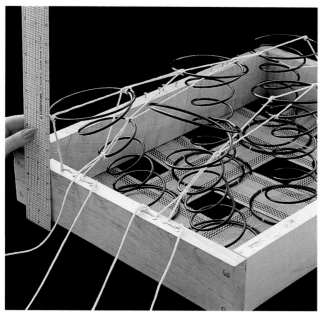

5) Pull one twine tail up to top coil of front spring; tie clove hitch knots around front and then back of top coil, tying spring at same height as center springs. Continue tying clove hitch knots, following diagram **(e),** page 43. Secure twine to rail, using another webbing nail. Repeat for each back-to-front-row.

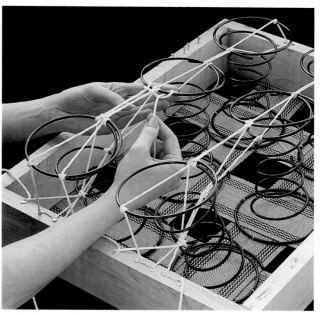

6) Pull remaining twine tail up to top coil of front spring. Tie clove hitch knot alongside first knot. Then tie knots over existing knots, following diagram **(e),** page 43.

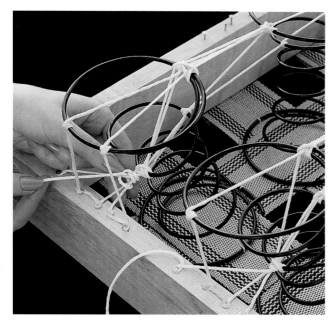

7) Tie several half hitch knots around twines between third coil and rail. Repeat for all back-to-front rows.

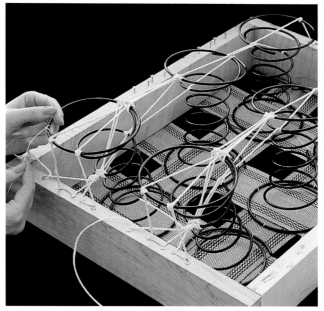

8) Cut piece of button twine, about 70" (178 cm) long. Spread knots on front top coil about 1½" (3.8 cm). Fold twine in half, tie clove hitch knot to coil just outside one knot.

(Continued on next page)

How to Tie Springs with an Edge Wire (continued)

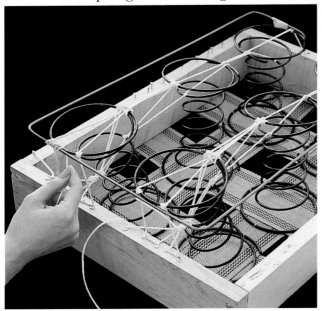

9) Align edge wire to outer edges of top coils. Wrap doubled button twine repeatedly around coil and edge wire, wrapping once outside knot, then crossing over knot and filling space between knots, and then crossing second knot and wrapping twice. Pack twines closely together in single layer.

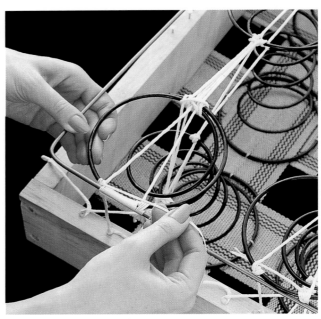

10) Wrap twines between spring and edge wire over previous wraps, pulling tight. Separate twines, and wrap them twice in opposite directions around spring and edge wire, forming figure eights; tie the ends together, using two overhand knots.

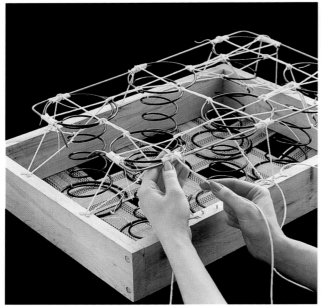

11) Repeat steps 8 to 10 at each spring. Set in nails for front side-to-side row, aligning nails to center of top coils. Tie side-to-side rows, following diagram **(f)** for first twine and diagram **(g)** for second twine; use clove hitch knots or overhand knots at each location for both twines, keeping all springs but front row perpendicular to webbing. Tie knots over any existing knots or loops.

12) Mark rails and prepare twines for diagonal rows as on page 37, step 8. Tie diagonal rows as in step 11, left, tying outer knots to edge wire. Cut twine tails to about 3" (7.5 cm).

How to Cover Springs with Burlap

1) Cut burlap 3" (7.5 cm) larger than measurements from outer edges of rails, over springs. Center burlap over spring system. Staple burlap to rails at center front and center back, using ⅜" (1 cm) staples and pulling snug without compressing springs. Repeat at center sides.

2) Finish stapling burlap on all sides, working from centers toward corners. Fold out excess burlap at corners; staple. Fold raw edge of burlap back; staple again.

3) Thread 6" (15 cm) curved needle with nylon button twine. Beginning with a corner spring, insert needle through burlap, hooking top coil. Take one short stitch, coming back through burlap, leaving tail for knotting. Secure stitch with slipknot. Tie overhand knot over slipknot.

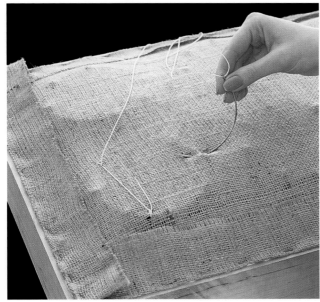

4) Stitch burlap to spring with two more evenly spaced stitches, arranging stitches so that last stitch is located near next spring. Secure each stitch with an overhand knot.

5) Secure burlap to each spring with three stitches, working one entire row; proceed to next row. Plan stitch placement so that last stitch on each spring is near first stitch on next spring. Lock all stitches between first and last stitch with overhand knots; lock last stitch with slipknot, followed by two overhand knots.

Diagrams for Spring Tying

Follow these diagrams for tying springs so that, when completed, the springs in the system will work together as one unit. For a domed surface spring system, the top coils of the springs around the outer edges should angle toward the front, back, and side rails. For an edge wire spring system, the top coils should all form a flat surface even with the edge wire. If open-ended coil springs are used, the second knot on the back springs in diagram **(c)** should also secure the open end to the coil beneath it.

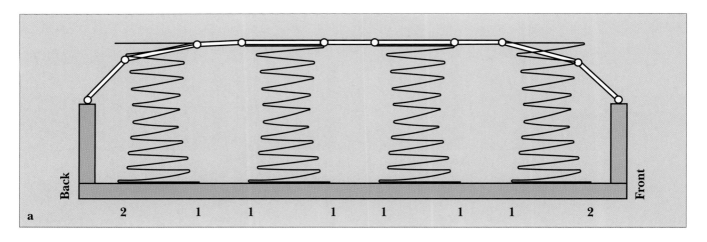

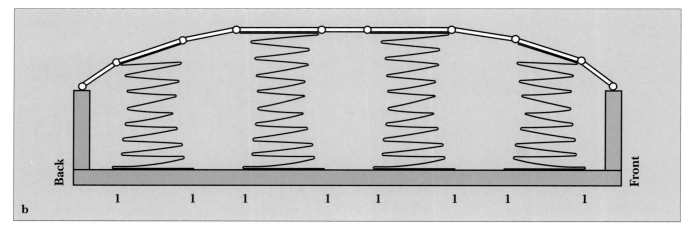

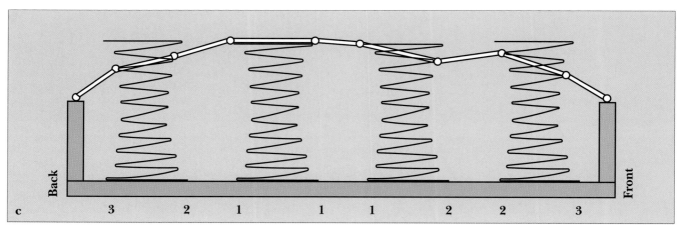

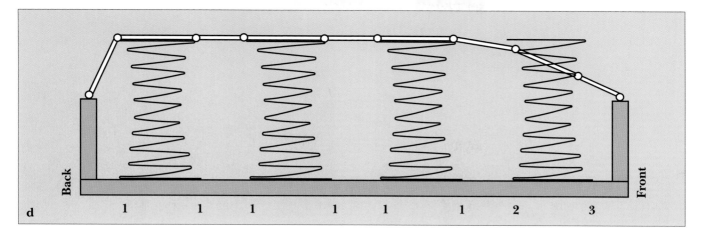

d

Back   1   1   1   1   1   1   2   3   Front

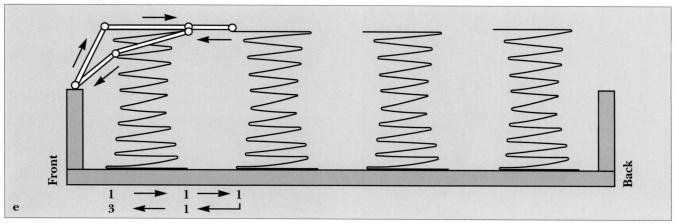

e

Front   1 → 1 → 1   Back

3 ← 1 ←

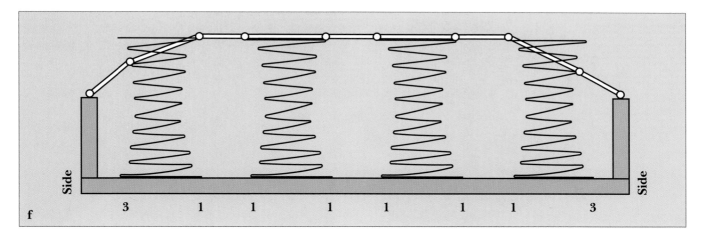

f

Side   3   1   1   1   1   1   1   3   Side

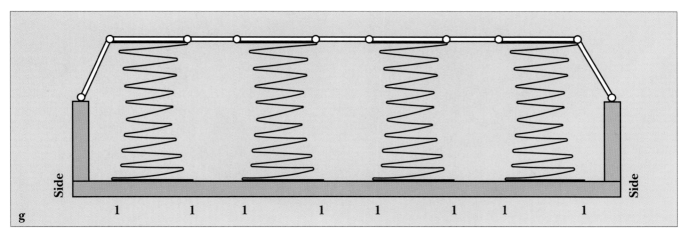

g

Side   1   1   1   1   1   1   1   1   Side

Welting

Fabric-covered cording, called *welting*, is both a decorative accent and a structural aspect of many upholstered pieces. Welting is attached along the lower edge of a chair to accent the edge and give it a clean finish. It is often sewn into the seam between two adjoining pieces, or stapled to the chair frame between two adjoining pieces. While accenting the structural lines of the furniture piece, it also reduces wear and stress at these locations.

To conserve fabric, welting strips can be cut on the crosswise grain of the fabric. Since the resulting welting will be quite inflexible, use straight-grain welting only in places where it is applied to the furniture piece in a straight line. For welting applied in a curve,

cut the strips on the bias, allowing the welting to bend without puckering. It is possible to use a combination of straight-grain and bias-grain welting in the same furniture piece, if the difference in grain cannot be detected.

Whenever possible, place welt seams and joints in inconspicuous places, such as the back of a cushion near a corner. Avoid placing them at the center of a section or on the front of the furniture piece.

Double welting is used as a decorative trim, often covering a raw fabric edge and staples or tacks. It is used in place of purchased trim, such as gimp.

Types of Welting

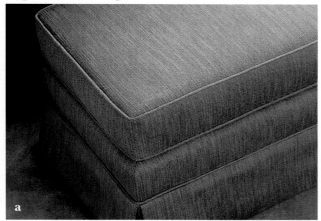

Welting can be made from matching or contrasting fabric, depending on the look desired. Matching welting (**a**) gives the piece an overall uniform appearance. Contrasting welting (**b**) visually divides the piece into smaller sections and emphasizes its design lines. Coordinating prints (**c**) or bias-cut

stripes can be used to add creative interest to welted upholstery. If upholstering with a stripe or plaid, keep in mind that it will not always be possible to match the welting to the fabric. It is better to cut self-welting on the bias (**d**) or to use a solid color for the welting.

How to Make Welting for Attaching to the Frame

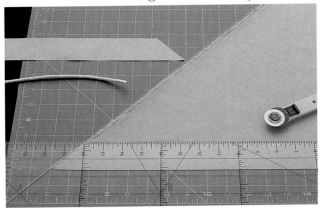

1) Cut fabric strips from bias grain or crosswise grain, with the width equal to the circumference of cording plus 1" (2.5 cm). Cut the short ends of strips at 45° angles for seaming.

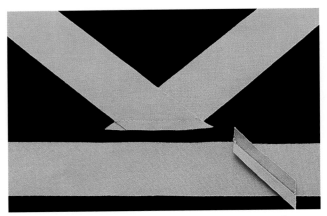

2) Stitch strips together as necessary for desired length; press seams open.

3) Center cording on wrong side of fabric strip; fold strip around cording, wrong sides together, matching raw edges and encasing cord.

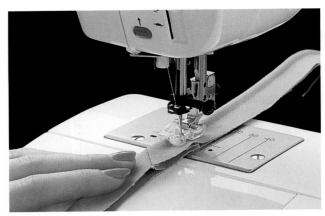

4) Machine-baste close to cording, using welting foot or zipper foot, to create welting.

How to Sew Welting into a Seam

Continuous circle. 1) Follow steps 1 to 3, above; align cut edges of welting strip to cut edge of the fabric, beginning 3" (7.5 cm) from end of welting. Stitch close to cording, using welting foot or zipper foot.

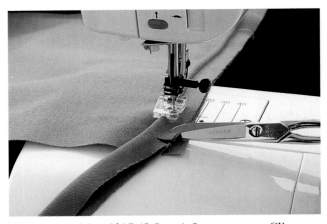

2) Stop stitching 1½" (3.8 cm) from corner. Clip welting seam allowances at corner and again ½" (1.3 cm) behind corner.

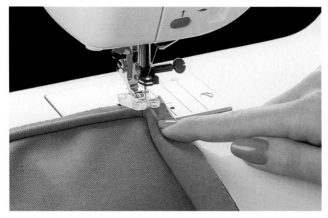

3) **Stitch** to corner. Leave needle down; raise presser foot, and pivot. Pull the welting completely back against itself, forming sharp corner. Realign welting to seamline.

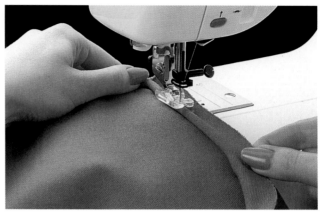

4) **Continue** stitching 2" (5 cm) beyond the corner. Leave needle down; raise presser foot. Hold welting seam allowances taut; push thumb into welting corner, drawing more cording back to fill out corner.

5) **Stop** stitching 3" (7.5 cm) from point where ends of welting will meet. Overlap welting strip ends; mark with chalk across both welt strips. Cut off welting strip ends ½" (1.3 cm) beyond marks.

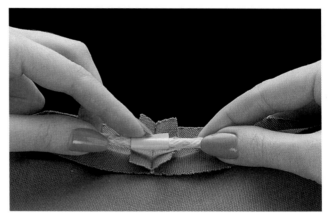

6) **Stitch** welt strip ends together at marked lines; finger-press seam open. Cut cording so ends butt. Wrap cording joint with tape; tuck cording back inside welting. Finish sewing welting to fabric.

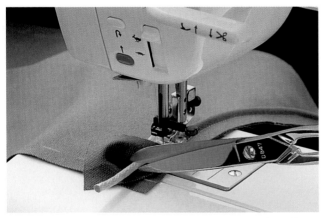

For welting that is crossed by a seam. 1) Stitch welting to edge of fabric, stopping 1" (2.5 cm) behind seam intersection. Cut off cording just behind seam intersection. Slip cording back into welting strip.

2) **Notch** welting seam allowance, starting ½" (1.3 cm) behind seam intersection. Bend welting down into the seam allowance, aligning upper edge of welting to seam intersection point. Finish stitching welting to fabric, stitching across empty welting.

Tips for Attaching Welting

Stretch welting slightly while stapling; slackness will cause rippling.

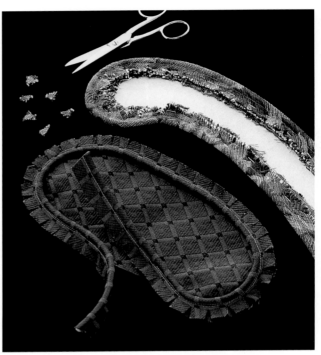

Clip welting seam allowances when they lie outside curves, allowing welting to lie flat. Notch seam allowances when they lie inside curves and corners, reducing bulk.

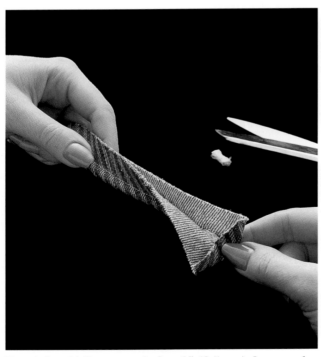

Butt joint. 1) Remove stitches 1" (2.5 cm) from end of welting. Open casing; cut off cording ½" (1.3 cm) from end. Turn back fabric over cording; refold, encasing cording. Staple welting in place.

2) Stop stapling 4" to 5" (10 to 12.5 cm) from joint. Cut off welting ½" (1.3 cm) beyond joint; remove stitches 1" (2.5 cm) from end of welting. Open casing; cut off cording ½" (1.3 cm) from end. Turn back fabric over cording; refold, encasing cording. Staple welting in place, butting ends tightly together.

How to Make Double Welting

1) **Place** 5/32" (3.8 mm) cording on wrong side of 3" (7.5 cm) fabric strip. Fold fabric over cording, with ½" (1.3 cm) seam allowance extending. Stitch next to cording, using welting foot or zipper foot.

2) **Place** second cording next to first welt. Wrap fabric around second cording.

3) **Stitch** between the two cords on previous stitching line. Use general-purpose foot, riding on top of the welting.

4) **Trim** off excess fabric next to stitching; raw edge is on the back of finished double welting.

Cushions

Cushions found on chairs, sofas, and ottomans vary in construction method and design. Three basic styles of cushions are boxed (a), waterfall (b), and knife-edge (c). Any of these may be fitted flush to the front of the chair or T-shaped, wrapping around the front of the chair arms. Boxed cushions can be sewn with or without welting at the top and bottom seams. Knife-edge cushions usually have a welted seam around the center on sides where the cushion is exposed. Hidden sides are often constructed with a boxing strip. Water-fall cushions, common in contemporary furniture, are sewn with one continuous piece of fabric wrapping over the front, from top to bottom. This style has a boxing strip around the sides and back and is usually constructed without welting.

As a general rule, the finished width of the boxing strip is ¾" (2 cm) narrower than the height of the foam. Many waterfall cushions, however, are made with narrower boxing strips. The fabric wraps over the sides from the top and bottom and forms small pleats around the curved front of the boxing strip. To copy this type of cushion cover, it is best to make a pattern off the original cushion.

Chair and sofa cushions are generally constructed with a zipper closure centered in the boxing strip that wraps around the back corners of the cushion. This allows for easier insertion of the cushion into its cover. Because the cushions must be shaped to conform to the back and sides of the chair or sofa, it is necessary to tailor a pattern before cutting the fabric. The pattern-tailoring instructions given are for single chair cushions. However, patterns for multiple sofa cushions are tailored in the same manner, marking the dividing line between cushions on the sofa deck and then making a separate pattern for each cushion.

Cushions that are exposed on all sides, such as otto-man cushions, are hand-sewn closed. These rectangular cushions, generally boxed or knife-edge, do not need a tailored pattern.

YOU WILL NEED

Muslin; chalk, for tailoring fitted pattern.

Upholstery fabric.

Welt cording; fabric, for making welting.

Upholstery zipper, or continuous zipper tape and zipper pull.

Foam.

Polyester batting; spray foam adhesive, or button needle and heavy thread.

Boxed Cushions

✂ Cutting Directions

Cut a cushion top and a cushion bottom, using the pattern tailored on page 52, steps 1 to 4. If making a rectangular cushion, exposed on all sides, cut a cushion top and a cushion bottom, with the length and width equal to the desired finished length and width plus 1" (2.5 cm). If the cushion will be welted, cut fabric strips for the welting (page 45), with the length equal to twice the circumference of the cushion plus additional length for seaming strips, joining ends, and inconspicuously positioning seams.

Cut the boxing strip. If the original cushion insert will be used, measure the width of the original boxing strip between the seams and add 1" (2.5 cm) for seam allowances. If a new cushion insert will be prepared, cut the boxing strip ¼" (6 mm) wider than the foam thickness. For a cushion that will be sewn closed, the cut length of the boxing strip is equal to the finished circumference of the cushion plus 1" (2.5 cm) for seam allowances. If seaming will be necessary, allow 1" (2.5 cm) for each seam, planning for inconspicuous placement.

For a cushion with a zipper closure, cut the boxing strip with the length equal to the measurement of the front and sides of the cushion. Excess length will be cut off during construction. If seaming will be necessary, allow 1" (2.5 cm) for each seam, planning the placement of the seams out of view along the sides of the cushion. If continuous zipper tape is used, cut the zipper tape with the length equal to the back cushion measurement plus 8" (20.5 cm), or purchase an upholstery zipper with this approximate length. Cut two fabric strips for the zipper closure, with the length of the strips equal to the length of the zipper tape and the width of the strips equal to half the cut width of the boxing strip plus ¾" (2 cm).

How to Tailor a Pattern for a Boxed Cushion

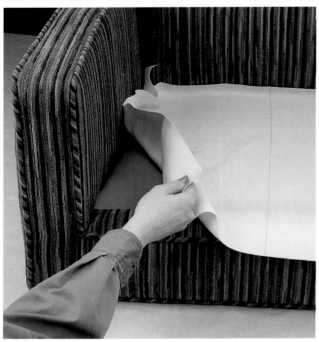

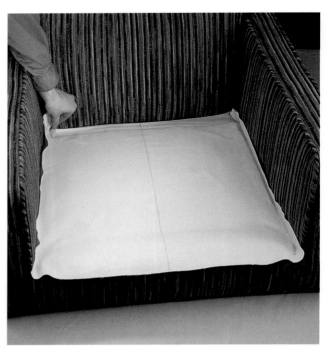

1) Measure the seat opening in both directions at the widest points; add 2" (5 cm) to each measurement. Cut muslin to this size; mark centerline from front to back. Center muslin over chair deck, turning excess muslin up along arms and back. For a T-cushion, clip muslin around curves, allowing it to lie flat.

2) Mark outline of cushion, holding sharpened stick of chalk perpendicular to deck and following shape of inside arms and back of chair; chalk should brush against but not push into chair padding. Mark cushion front along crown of nosing.

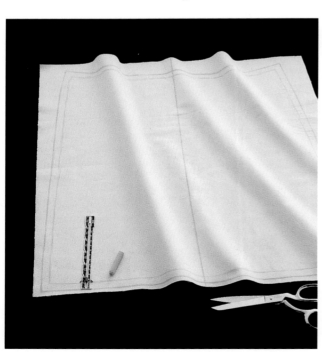

3) Remove muslin. Draw ½" (1.3 cm) seam allowance outside marked line; cut out pattern.

4) Fold pattern in half on centerline, checking to see that pattern is symmetrical. Trim edges even if they are off by less than 1" (2.5 cm); unfold pattern. If edges are off by more than 1" (2.5 cm), adjust chair padding and draw new pattern.

How to Sew a Boxed Cushion Cover with a Zipper

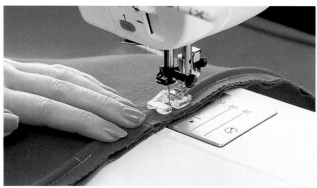

1) **Sew** welting around outer edges of cushion top and cushion bottom, following the continuous circle method on pages 46 and 47, steps 1 to 6.

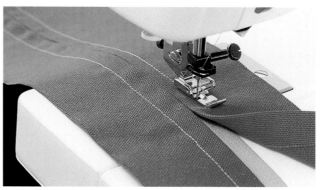

2) **Press** under ¾" (2 cm) seam allowance on one long edge of zipper strip. Position folded edge of strip along center of zipper teeth, right sides up. Using zipper foot, topstitch ⅜" (1 cm) from fold. Repeat for opposite side, making sure folds meet at center of zipper. If using continuous zipper tape, attach zipper pull to tape.

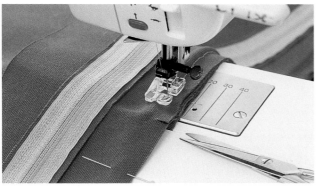

3) **Center** the zipper strip over back of cushion top. Stitch zipper strip to cushion top, beginning and ending on sides about 1½" (3.8 cm) beyond corners; clip once into zipper strip seam allowance at each corner, and pivot.

4) **Align** center of boxing strip to front center of cushion top, matching print, if necessary; pin-mark pieces separately. Smooth boxing strip to right front corner; mark with ⅜" (1 cm) clip into seam allowance. Smooth boxing strip along right side of cushion top; pin boxing strip to cushion top about 6" (15 cm) from back corner.

5) **Stitch** boxing strip to cushion top, beginning at side pin and sewing ½" (1.3 cm) seam. For welted cushion, use welting foot or zipper foot. Match clip mark to front corner; pivot stitching at corner.

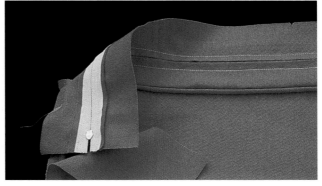

6) **Continue** stitching boxing strip to cushion top, matching center marks. Clip once into boxing strip seam allowance at left front corner; pivot. Stop stitching about 6" (15 cm) from back left corner.

(Continued on next page)

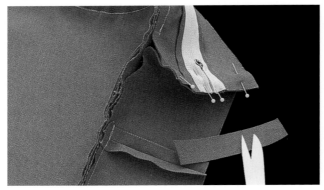

7) Cut boxing strip 4" (10 cm) beyond point where it overlaps zipper pull end of zipper strip. Pin end of boxing strip to end of zipper strip, right sides together, matching all cut edges.

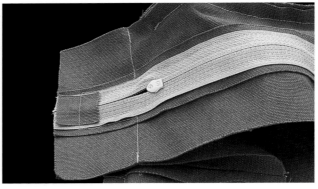

8) Stitch together 2" (5 cm) from end; pivot at zipper tape. Stitch along outer edge of zipper tape to within ½" (1.3 cm) of end; pivot. Place small scrap of fabric over zipper teeth. Stitch slowly across teeth to opposite side of zipper tape, taking care not to break needle; pivot. Stitch along opposite side of zipper tape until 2" (5 cm) from end; pivot, and stitch to edge.

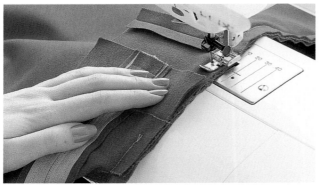

9) Finger-press seam allowance toward boxing strip; finish sewing zipper strip and boxing strip to the cushion top. Small pocket forms to hide zipper pull when closed.

10) Cut opposite end of boxing strip 1" (2.5 cm) beyond point where it overlaps end of zipper strip. Pin ends together. Stitch ½" (1.3 cm) from ends, placing scrap of fabric over the zipper teeth and stitching slowly. Turn seam allowance toward boxing strip; finish sewing zipper strip and boxing strip to cushion top.

11) Fold boxing strip straight across at corner; mark opposite side of boxing strip with ⅜" (1 cm) clip into seam allowance. Repeat for all corners.

12) Open zipper partially. Pin boxing strip to the cushion bottom, matching clip marks to corners. Stitch. Turn right side out through zipper opening.

How to Sew a Boxed Cushion Cover without a Zipper

1) Follow step 1 on page 53. Sew boxing strip sections together as necessary.

2) Check to see that boxing strip fits cushion top. Mark boxing strip at corners with ⅜" (1 cm) clips into seam allowance. Fold boxing strip straight across at marks; clip-mark opposite side of boxing strip.

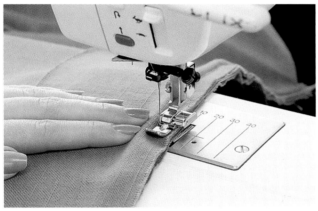

3) Pin boxing strip to cushion top, matching clip marks to corners; stitch ½" (1.3 cm) seam. Use welting foot or zipper foot if cushion is welted.

4) Pin boxing strip to cushion bottom, matching clip marks to corners; stitch ½" (1.3 cm) seam, leaving back side open for inserting cushion. Backstitch at beginning and end of seam.

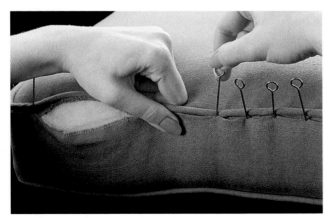

5) Prepare and insert cushion (pages 59 to 61). Fold back boxing strip seam allowance along opening, overlapping cushion bottom seam allowance ½" (1.3 cm); pin. Compress cushion along open side for easier pinning.

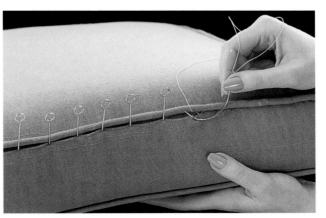

6) Blindstitch (page 69) opening closed, using 3" (7.5 cm) curved needle and heavy thread. Begin and end stitching 1" (2.5 cm) beyond opening; knot securely.

Waterfall Cushions

How to Tailor a Pattern for a Waterfall Cushion

✂ Cutting Directions

Cut a cushion top and bottom piece, using the pattern tailored in steps 1 to 3, right and below. Mark the end of the piece that will become the cushion top; with a directional print or napped fabric, the fabric will run in the correct direction only on the top.

Cut the side boxing strips. If the original cushion insert will be used, measure the width of the original boxing strip between the seams and add 1" (2.5 cm) for seam allowances. If a new cushion insert will be prepared, cut the boxing strips ¼" (6 mm) wider than the foam thickness. Cut each boxing strip with the length equal to the side measurement of the cushion plus 1" (2.5 cm). Excess length will be cut off during construction. If continuous zipper tape is used, cut the zipper tape with the length equal to the back cushion measurement plus 8" (20.5 cm), or purchase an upholstery zipper with this approximate length. Cut two fabric strips for the zipper closure, with the length of the strips equal to the length of the zipper tape and the width of the strips equal to half the cut width of the boxing strip plus ¾" (2 cm).

1) Measure the seat opening in both directions at the widest points. Multiply the depth by two and add the cushion height. Add 4" (10 cm) to the depth and 2" (5 cm) to the width measurements; cut muslin to this size. Mark centerline through entire length. Fold fabric in half, perpendicular to centerline; crease.

2) Draw a line across width of muslin a distance above fold equal to half the cushion height. Unfold muslin. Center one end of muslin over chair deck, aligning marked line to crown of nosing and turning excess muslin up along arms and back. For a T-cushion, clip muslin around curves, allowing it to lie flat.

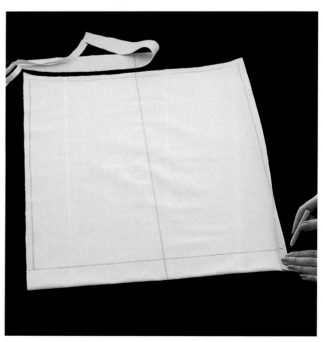

3) Follow steps 2 to 4 on page 52. Fold under uncut end of pattern along crosswise crease; cut lower layer to match cutting line of upper layer. Mark lower layer even with nosing line; unfold pattern.

How to Sew a Waterfall Cushion Cover

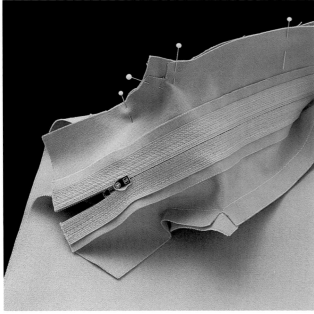

1) Follow steps 2 and 3 on page 53. Fold zipper strip straight across at corner; mark opposite edge with ⅜" (1 cm) clip into seam allowance. Repeat at other corner. Pin zipper strip to cushion bottom, matching clip marks to corners. Stitch, beginning and ending about 1½" (3.8 cm) beyond corners.

2) Mark the center of front short end of each side boxing strip; round front corners of the side boxing strips slightly. Mark outer edges of top and bottom cushion piece even with crosswise crease of pattern. Staystitch scant ½" (1.3 cm) from outer edges of piece a distance on either side of marks equal to the cushion height.

3) Clip seam allowances to staystitching every ½" (1.3 cm). Pin side boxing strip to cushion piece, right sides together, aligning center marks. Check to see that corresponding points on top and bottom match up directly across from each other on boxing strip. Sew ½" (1.3 cm) seam, beginning and ending 6" (15 cm) from back corners. Repeat for opposite side.

4) Follow steps 7 to 10 on page 54. Open the zipper partially. Finish sewing boxing strip to cushion bottom on both sides. Turn the cushion cover right side out through zipper opening.

Knife-edge Cushions

✂ Cutting Directions

Cut a cushion top and a cushion bottom, using the pattern tailored below for a fitted chair or sofa cushion. If the cushion is exposed on all four sides, cut two rectangles of fabric, with the width and length equal to the finished width and length of the cushion plus the foam height plus ¼" (6 mm). Cut fabric strips for the welting (page 45), with length equal to the length of the knife-edge section of the cushion cover.

Cut the side boxing strips. If the original cushion insert will be used, measure the width of the original boxing strip between the seams and add 1" (2.5 cm)

for seam allowances. If a new cushion insert will be prepared, cut the boxing strips ¼" (6 mm) wider than the foam thickness. Cut the boxing strips with the length equal to the measurement of the side of the cushion. Excess length will be cut off during construction. If continuous zipper tape is used, cut the zipper tape with the length equal to the back cushion measurement plus 8" (20.5 cm), or purchase an upholstery zipper with this approximate length. Cut two fabric strips for the zipper closure, with the length of the strips equal to the length of the zipper tape and the width of the strips equal to half the cut width of the boxing strip plus ¾" (2 cm).

How to Tailor a Pattern for a Knife-edge Cushion

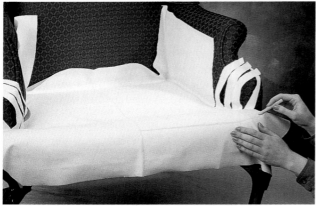

1) Follow steps 1 and 2 on page 52, adding the cushion height plus 2" (5 cm) to the seat measurements before cutting muslin. Remove muslin.

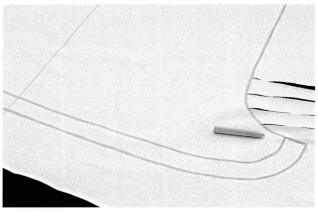

2) Draw line along the front of cushion pattern a distance from marked line equal to half the finished boxing height. For T-cushion, extend line around front corners to a point even with line at back of T; connect ends of lines.

3) Draw ½" (1.3 cm) seam allowance outside entire pattern; cut out pattern. Follow step 4 on page 52.

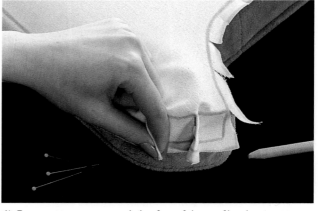

4) Lay pattern over original cushion, aligning pattern seamline to midpoint of cushion height; pin out corner tucks. Mark tucks; unfold pattern. Transfer marks to opposite corner.

How to Sew a Knife-edge Cushion Cover

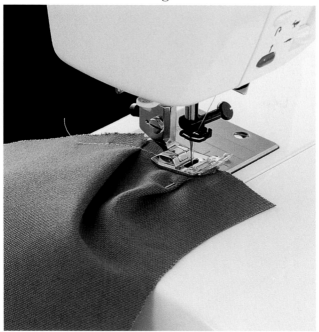

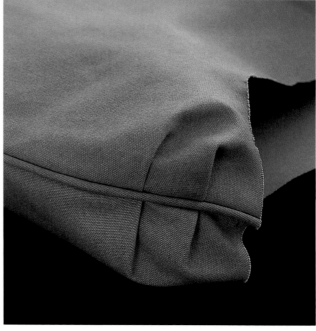

1) **Fold** out corner tucks on cushion top and bottom; baste. Sew welting to desired edges of cushion top, following the method for welting that is crossed by a seam on page 47, for tailored cushion, or the continuous circle method on pages 46 and 47, for totally knife-edged cushion.

2) **Pin** cushion bottom to cushion top along welted edge, matching corner tucks. Stitch seam, crowding cording. For totally knife-edged cushion, leave one side open for inserting cushion; hand-stitch closed. For tailored cushion, complete cushion cover as for waterfall cushion on page 57, steps 1 to 4.

How to Prepare and Insert the Cushion

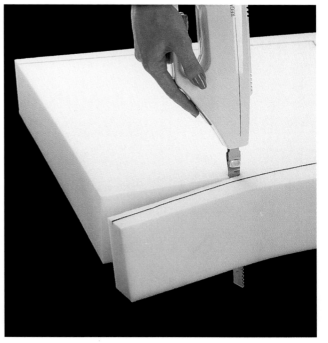

1) **Trace** cutting line of cushion cover onto foam, using marker.

2) **Cut** foam, using electric knife. Follow seamline of pattern for high-resiliency foam; follow cutting line for softer foam. Hold knife blade perpendicular to foam at all times.

(Continued on next page)

How to Prepare and Insert the Cushion (continued)

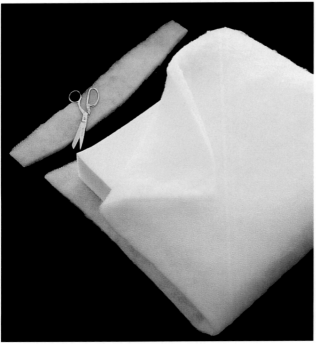

3) Wrap polyester batting over foam from front to back. Trim sides and back so that cut edges overlap about 1" (2.5 cm) at center of cushion.

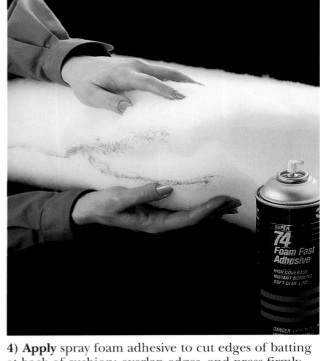

4) Apply spray foam adhesive to cut edges of batting at back of cushion; overlap edges, and press firmly to seal, forming smooth seam. Or whipstitch edges together, using button needle and heavy thread. Repeat for sides.

5) Trim excess batting vertically at back corners, for fitted cushion. Fold back excess batting over side seams at front corners of fitted cushion or all corners of rectangular cushion. Apply adhesive; press together firmly to seal. Or whipstitch corners in place.

6) Fold cushion in half from front to back. Insert into opening, gradually working cushion toward front of cover. Stretch cover to fit cushion.

7) Stand the cushion on one side. Check to see that cushion is inserted symmetrically, with equal fullness on both sides; adjust, if necessary.

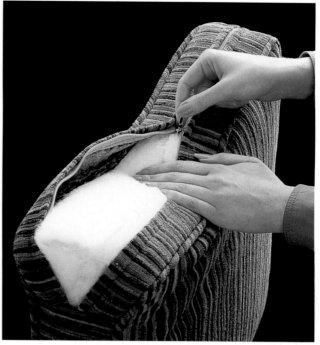

8) Turn seam allowances toward boxing strip all around cushion. Zip closed, hiding zipper pull in pocket. Or hand-stitch closed (page 55).

How to Insert the Cushion Using the Vacuum Method

1) Insert prepared cushion into lightweight trash bag, or wrap with lightweight plastic. Overlap open edges of plastic at one end. Insert vacuum hose into small hole cut in plastic bag, or wrap plastic around hose; hold tightly.

2) Place end of hose against cushion. Turn on the vacuum. Suck air from cushion until it slips easily into cover. Turn off vacuum; remove plastic, allowing air to reenter cushion.

a

b

c

d

Skirts

The final upholstery step for many furniture pieces is attaching a skirt around the bottom. Skirts add a decorative touch while also hiding plain legs and visually anchoring the furniture.

Skirt styles vary, depending on the design of the furniture and the look desired. The most common skirt style is a tailored, flat panel with kick pleats at the corners **(a)**. With this skirt style, the fabric pattern can be matched in a continuous flow to the floor. On larger pieces, such as a sofa, the tailored skirt may have one or two kick pleats along the front panel, aligned to the cushion breaks. Other skirt styles feature open box pleats **(b)** or closed box pleats **(c)** spaced evenly and continuously around the bottom. For a country or feminine look, the skirt can be gathered **(d)**. This style requires lightweight upholstery fabric.

The skirt is sewn to welting that fits tightly around the furniture. The entire skirt is then either hand-sewn or stapled in place. Though hand sewing seems more difficult and time-consuming, it results in a very attractive, secure finish. Stapling is only possible if the welt rests over unpadded or lightly padded wood.

Skirt length is very critical. Measure for the length with the furniture standing on a hard surface. The skirt hem should be ½" to 1" (1.3 to 2.5 cm) above the surface, if the furniture will be placed on a hard floor. If the furniture will be placed on a carpeted floor, depending on the depth of the pile, the skirt hem should be 1" to 1½" (2.5 to 3.8 cm) above the surface.

The placement for the upper welted edge of the skirt is usually determined by the original skirt placement. However, this can often be altered if a different look is desired. In general, the skirt should be at least 6" (15 cm) long. It may be helpful to pin a mock skirt at different heights to decide on the most appealing placement. Matching furniture pieces, such as a chair and ottoman, should always have matching skirts.

✂ Cutting Directions

For all skirt styles, cut fabric strips for the welting (page 45), with the length equal to the circumference of the furniture piece at the placement line for the upper edge of the skirt plus additional length for seaming strips, joining ends, and inconspicuously positioning seams.

For a flat-panel skirt, measure and record the widths of the front, back, and sides of the furniture piece, measuring along the skirt placement line as drawn on page 64, step 5. For a sofa, measure and record the distances from the corners to the first cushion breaks and the distance between any additional cushion breaks. Cut a separate piece of fabric for each section of the skirt, with the width equal to the measured width of the section plus 8" (20.5 cm). The cut length of each section is equal to the desired finished length of the skirt from the welt seam to the hem plus 1½" (3.8 cm). Follow the pattern-matching guidelines on page 22 for cutting patterned fabric.

Cut a piece of fabric, 8" (20.5 cm) wide, for the underpanel of each kick pleat, with the length of each piece equal to the cut length of the skirt sections.

Cut lining pieces equal in width to each skirt section and underpanel; the cut length of the lining pieces is 1" (2.5 cm) shorter than the cut length of the skirt.

Cut buckram pieces for each skirt section and underpanel, with the cut width equal to the finished width of the section minus ½" (1.3 cm) and the cut length equal to the finished length of the skirt minus ¾" (2 cm).

For a box-pleated or gathered skirt, measure the circumference of the furniture piece, measuring along the skirt placement line as drawn on page 64, step 5. Cut fabric pieces with the total cut width, after seaming, of two-and-one-half times this measurement for open box pleats or gathers or three times this measurement for closed box pleats. The cut length of the pieces is equal to the desired finished length of the skirt from the welting seam to the hem plus 1½" (3.8 cm).

Cut lining equal in width, after seaming to the cut width of the skirt, railroading (page 17) lining to eliminate some seams, if possible. The cut length of the lining is 1" (2.5 cm) shorter than the cut length of the skirt.

YOU WILL NEED

Upholstery fabric.

Lining fabric, such as lightweight denim.

Buckram, for tailored flat-panel skirt.

Welt cording.

Chalk, for marking placement line.

#3 curved needle and heavy thread or staple gun and ⅜" (1 cm) staples, for attaching the skirt.

How to Sew a Tailored Flat-panel Skirt

1) Pin lining to lower edge of one skirt section, matching cut edges; stitch ½" (1.3 cm) seam.

2) Press seam allowances toward lining. Understitch on right side of lining, close to seamline, stitching through lining and both seam allowances.

3) Pin lining and fabric, right sides together, at ends; align upper and side edges. Skirt fabric will roll ½" (1.3 cm) toward the lining side. Stitch ½" (1.3 cm) seam. Repeat for opposite end.

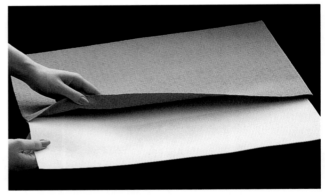

4) Turn skirt section right side out, aligning upper edges; press. Insert buckram between skirt and lining, aligning lower edge of buckram to bottom of skirt. Baste upper edges of skirt and lining together within ½" (1.3 cm) seam allowance.

5) Repeat steps 1 to 4 for all skirt sections and pleat underpanels. Determine placement for top of skirt; mark with chalk at height of welting seam, measuring up from floor. Make welting as on page 46, steps 1 to 4.

6) Wrap welting tightly around furniture at marked line, lapping ends at the back; pin. Check to see that welting seams are placed inconspicuously. Pin-mark welting at corners and at cushion breaks, if any. Mark ends at overlap.

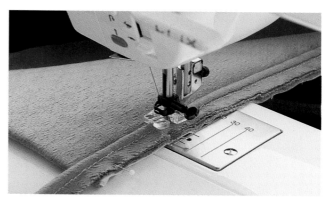

7) Remove welting. Cut off welting strip ends ½" (1.3 cm) beyond marks. Join ends as on page 47, step 6; sew welting closed, forming circle.

8) Fold under 3½" (9 cm) at ends of front skirt panel. Pin welting to panel, aligning seam allowances and matching front pin marks to folds. Adjust depth of folds, if necessary. Stitch, welting side up, using welting foot or zipper foot and crowding cording. Repeat for each skirt section.

9) Press folds. Center pleat underpanel over folds at one corner, right sides down. Shift underpanel upward, ¼" to ⅜" (6 mm to 1 cm) beyond upper edges of skirt and welting seam allowance; stitch.

10) Turn welting seam allowance toward kick pleat; check to see that lower edge of underpanel is even with or slightly shorter than lower edges of corner folds. Adjust, if necessary. Repeat step 9 for remaining kick pleats, shifting underpanel same distance as for first corner.

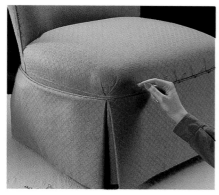

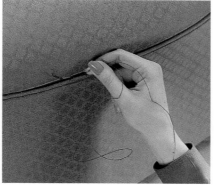

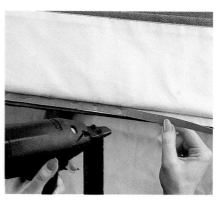

11) Slip skirt onto furniture from bottom, first over back legs and then over front. Turn down upper seam allowances; align welting seamline to marked line on furniture; pin.

12) Blindstitch (page 69) skirt to furniture, using #3 curved needle and heavy thread, stitching into welting seam.

Stapled method. 12) Turn the skirt up. Place tack strip over the seam allowances, aligning upper edge of the tack strip to seamline. Staple in place.

How to Sew a Gathered Skirt

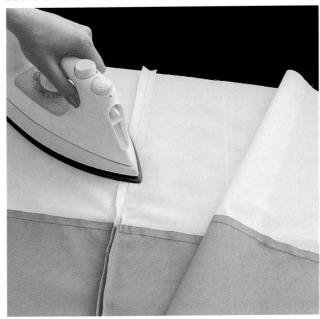

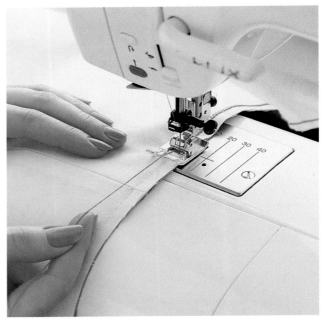

1) Seam skirt and lining as necessary to obtain the desired cut width; press seam allowances open. Sew lining to skirt as on page 64, steps 1 and 2. Sew ends, right sides together, making continuous circle; press seam allowances open.

2) Fold skirt, wrong sides together, aligning upper cut edges; baste within ½" (1.3 cm) seam allowance, taking care not to let layers shift. Zigzag over a cord within seam allowance on back side of skirt. Mark furniture and prepare the welting as on pages 64 and 65, steps 5 to 7.

3) Measure distance between two welting pin marks, beginning at a back corner. Pin-mark upper edge of skirt, measuring 2½ times this distance; place first pin about 3" (7.5 cm) from seam. Repeat for all pin-marked sections; measurements on skirt need not be exact.

4) Pin welting to right side of skirt, matching pin marks. Pull on the gathering cord, and gather skirt evenly to fit welting.

5) Sew welting to the skirt, using welting foot or zipper foot. Attach skirt to furniture as on page 65, steps 11 and 12.

How to Sew a Pleated Skirt

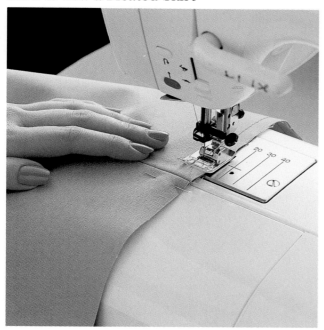

1) Prepare skirt as in step 1, opposite. Fold skirt, wrong sides together, aligning upper cut edges; baste within ½" (1.3 cm) seam allowance, taking care not to let layers shift.

2) Measure distance between two welting pin marks, beginning at a back corner. Pin-mark upper edge of skirt, measuring 2½ times this distance for open box pleats or 3 times this distance for closed box pleats; place first pin about 2" (5 cm) from seam. Repeat for all pin-marked sections; measurements on skirt need not be exact.

3) Determine the desired size and spacing of pleats. Fold out pleats, hiding any seams in the folds of the pleats. For open box pleats, pleat sequence on front and back begins and ends with a fold; pleat sequence on sides begins and ends with a space. For closed box pleats, position folds at all corners.

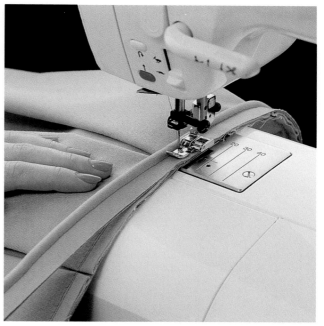

4) Pin welting to skirt, matching pin marks on the welting to skirt corners; stitch, using welting foot or zipper foot. Attach skirt to furniture as on page 65, steps 11 and 12.

Hand-stitch around the front arm band of a rolled arm, using small, evenly spaced running stitches. Pull up on thread to pleat out fabric evenly; staple.

Fitting & Finishing Techniques

Molding flat pieces of fabric over padded curves while circumventing numerous rails and posts is not a hit-or-miss procedure. Upholstery is actually a methodical craft, which, once understood, makes perfect sense. The secret to achieving professional results lies in the correct application of a few basic upholstery techniques.

Stitch *stretchers,* strips of strong, inexpensive fabric, to the edges of a cover section that will be hidden, conserving upholstery fabric. Turn seam allowances toward stretcher; edgestitch. Attach the section to the furniture frame as usual, making necessary cuts and stapling through the stretchers.

Staple-baste the cover fabric to hold it in place temporarily, while working in another area. Hold the staple gun just above the surface; drive the staple partway into the frame, allowing it to be easily removed before final stapling.

Steam the newly upholstered furniture, shrinking out any minute puckers and tightening the cover for a taut, firm appearance.

Pleat out excess fabric to make cover fit smoothly around convex curves, such as the rounded back of an overstuffed chair. Use a regulator (page 11) to form sharp pleats.

Prevent pull marks by stapling just behind, rather than directly over, the spot being pulled. Stapling through padding also produces pull marks.

Relief-cut the edge of cover fabric with a series of cuts, allowing it to mold smoothly around a concave curve, such as the inward arc of a wing. Make the cuts shallow enough so that they will be covered by an adjoining cover section, but deep enough to be effective. Depending on the location and shape of the curve, the relief cuts may consist of evenly spaced clips along the cut edge (**a**) or a series of clips that branch off from each other (**b**).

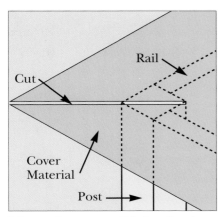

Diagonal-cut cover fabric, allowing it to wrap around opposite sides of a corner post. Measure before cutting to ensure that the cut will end at inside corner of post. Fold under cut edges even with post sides; pull taut, and staple to rails.

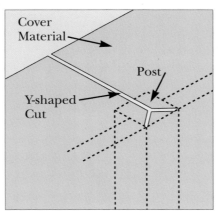

Y-cut cover fabric, allowing it to wrap around opposite sides of a post or rail that is not at a corner. The width of the Y is equal to the width of the post or rail. Measure before cutting to ensure that the cut will end at face of post or rail.

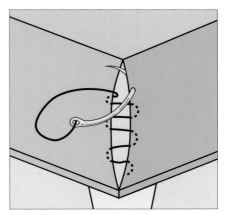

Blindstitch adjoining sections together when other methods of attachment are not suitable. Use a curved needle to stitch in and out of the adjoining pieces, once they are pinned in place.

Upholstery
Projects

Slip Seats

Upholstered seats on dining room or kitchen chairs are often referred to as slip seats. Because they are so easy to remove and reupholster, slip seats are a good choice for a beginning project. Whether the seat is worn or soiled, or if you simply want to change the fabric to coordinate with the room, a set of four chairs can easily be reupholstered in a day.

Most slip seats are made of a thin board, usually padded with foam and polyester batting. Another style of slip seat consists of an open wooden framework with a webbed top. The webbing is covered with burlap, and the seat may be padded with either horsehair and cotton batting or foam and polyester batting. If the padding is in good condition and the webbing is still taut, the chair seats can be reupholstered simply by removing the outer cover and attaching new fabric, as on page 74, steps 4 to 10. If the webbing is slack, the padding must be removed and the seat rewebbed (page 28). New foam and polyester batting can be attached, as on page 74, steps 2 and 3.

The slip seats of some chair styles drop into a recess in the chair seat. Other styles rest directly on the surface of the seat and may have welting attached around the lower edge. All styles are held in place by screws attached from the underside of the seat. Regardless of the style, if more than one chair in a set is being reupholstered, it is important to return seats to their original chairs, assuring proper fit and alignment of screw holes.

✂ Cutting Directions

Cut the fabric 6" (15 cm) larger than the length and width of the chair seat. If new padding is needed, cut the foam 1" (2.5 cm) larger than the length and width of the chair seat. Cut the batting roughly 4" (10 cm) larger than the length and width of the chair seat. Cut the cambric 2" (5 cm) larger than the chair seat.

For the welting at the bottom of the chair seat, cut fabric strips 1½" (3.8 cm) wide on either the bias or crosswise grain; the combined length of the strips is equal to the distance around the chair seat plus extra for seam allowances and butt joint.

YOU WILL NEED

Screwdriver; tack lifter or staple remover.

Foam, 1" (2.5 cm) thick.

Foam adhesive.

Polyester upholstery batting, 27" (68.5 cm) wide; 3 yd. (2.75 m) is sufficient for four chair seats.

Webbing and webbing stretcher, to replace webbing on webbed slip seat, optional.

Upholstery fabric.

Staple gun and ⅜" (1 cm) **staples.**

Welt cording, 5/32" (3.8 mm) diameter, for welting, optional.

Cambric, for underside of chair seat, optional; 2 yd. (1.85 m) is sufficient for four chair seats.

How to Upholster a Slip Seat

1) Remove screws on underside of seat; remove seat. Strip off existing outer fabric, using staple remover or tack lifter. If the foundation is intact, omit steps 2 and 3.

2) Apply spray adhesive to one side of foam; affix foam to top of seat.

3) Place upholstery batting on table; place seat, foam side down, over batting. Wrap batting around top and sides of seat. Trim excesss batting even with the bottom edge of seat.

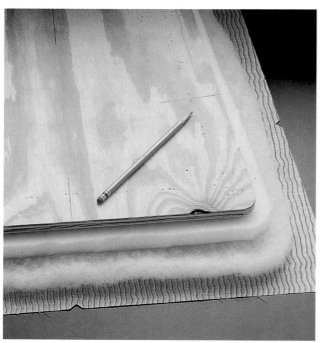 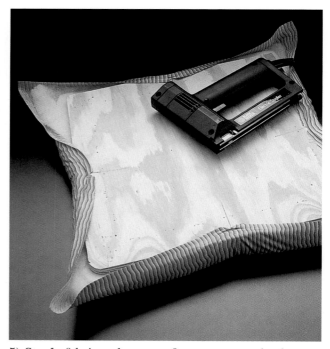

4) Mark center of each side on bottom of seat. Notch center of each side of fabric. Place fabric on table, wrong side up. Center the seat upside down over the fabric.

5) Staple fabric to bottom of seat at center back, matching center marks. Stretch fabric from back to front; staple at center front, matching the center marks. Repeat at center of each side.

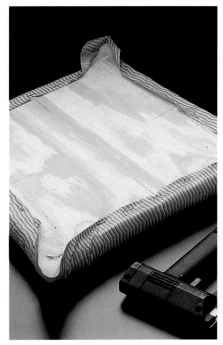

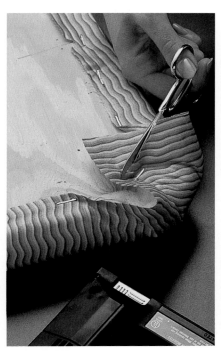

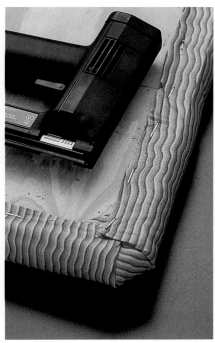

6) Apply staples to back of seat at 1½" (3.8 cm) intervals, working from center toward sides, to within 3" (7.5 cm) of corners. Pull fabric taut toward front of seat; staple. Repeat for sides.

7) Fold fabric diagonally at corner; stretch the fabric taut, and staple between screw hole and corner. Trim excess fabric diagonally across the corner.

8) Miter fabric at corner by folding in each side up to corner; staple in place. Repeat for remaining corners. Trim excess fabric, exposing screw holes. If welting is not desired, omit step 9. If cambric is not desired, omit step 10.

9) Make welting as on page 46, steps 1 to 4. Staple welting around seat at ¾" (2 cm) intervals, starting at back of seat; align stitching line of welting to edge of seat. Follow tips on page 48.

10) Fold under raw edges of cambric; staple to bottom of seat at 1" (2.5 cm) intervals. Puncture cambric at screw holes in the chair seat. Screw upholstered seat to chair.

Carved-wood Footstools

Among the great finds at antique stores are footstools with lovely carved-wood frames. If the frame is still in good condition, the footstool can be restored to like-new condition by replacing the upholstery. Covered with a traditional fabric, such as tapestry or hand-stitched needlepoint, and trimmed with contrasting gimp or decorative nails, the footstool becomes a handsome room accessory.

The style shown here has a webbed base, originally covered with padding: possibly hair, cotton, or even straw. If the footstool originally had a spring foundation, with the webbing attached to the underside of the frame, you may wish to attach new webbing (page 28) and retie the springs (page 32). For the easiest method of upholstery, however, attach new webbing to the upper side of the frame and pad the top with foam and batting.

YOU WILL NEED

Decorator fabric, such as tapestry fabric, or hand-stitched needlepoint.

Webbing and webbing stretcher.

Foam in 1" (2.5 cm) thickness; aerosol foam adhesive.

Polyester upholstery batting.

Burlap, for support under the foam.

Cambric, for dustcover on bottom of footstool.

Gimp trim; use gimp that matches fabric if decorative upholstery nails are being applied over the gimp, or use matching or contrasting color if gimp is used alone as a decorative edging.

Decorative upholstery nails, optional; upholstery hammer for inserting decorative nails.

Staple gun; 3⁄8" or 1⁄2" (1 or 1.3 cm) staples.

Hot glue gun and glue sticks.

How to Upholster a Footstool

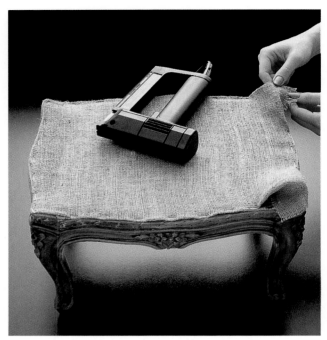

1) Strip all layers of old fabric, padding, burlap, and webbing from the stool; remove all decorative nails and tacks. Refinish wood frame, if necessary.

2) Attach webbing to upper side of the frame as on pages 30 and 31, steps 1 to 6. Cut burlap 3" (7.5 cm) larger than the footstool frame. Fold under edge of burlap piece; staple it to the top of the frame, over the webbing, at 1½" (3.8 cm) intervals, stretching burlap taut.

3) Place the footstool upside down on foam; draw outline of frame on foam, using pencil. Cut foam ½" (1.3 cm) beyond the marked lines, using scissors.

4) Apply aerosol adhesive to marked side of foam and to the burlap. Place the footstool upside down on foam, pressing down so foam adheres to the burlap. Stand footstool right side up; press down on foam.

5) Place a layer of upholstery batting over the foam, wrapping it around the sides of footstool; trim excess batting above the decorative wood.

6) Measure footstool length and width from decorative wood on one side, over foam and batting, to decorative wood on opposite side. Add 5" (12.5 cm) to these measurements; cut decorator fabric to this size.

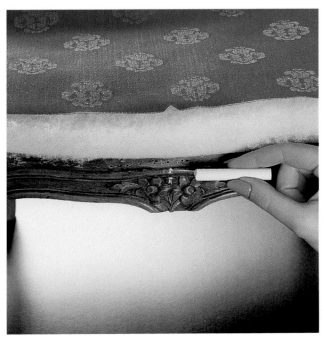

7) Notch the center of each side of the fabric; mark decorative wood on center of each side of footstool frame, using chalk.

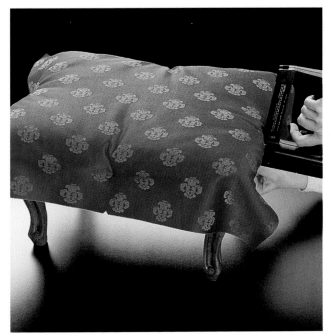

8) Place fabric, right side up, over batting. Staple-baste center of fabric at center on front of frame, just above decorative wood, then at center on back of frame, stretching fabric slightly. Repeat in other direction, staple-basting fabric at center of each side.

(Continued on next page)

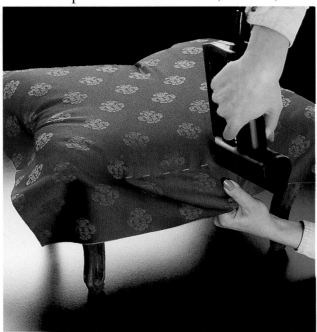

9) Remove the center staple from front of frame; stretch the fabric taut, and staple again at center. Working from center toward one side, apply staples at 1" (2.5 cm) intervals, stretching fabric taut; stop 3" (7.5 cm) from corner. Repeat, working from center toward opposite side.

10) Repeat step 9 on back of the footstool, stretching fabric taut; then repeat for sides of stool.

11) Stretch fabric at corner, dividing excess fullness equally on each side of corner; insert one staple, centered above the leg, just above decorative wood.

12) Fold fabric as shown, forming an inverted pleat, or "V," at the corner, folding out all excess fabric. Staple in place. Repeat at remaining corners.

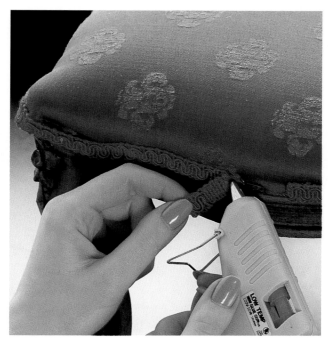

13) Finish stapling each side at 1" (2.5 cm) intervals, up to corners, stretching the fabric taut. Trim excess fabric on all sides of the footstool, just above the decorative wood.

14) Glue gimp above the decorative wood, using hot glue gun, starting at center of one side; make sure that the raw edges and staples are covered. Fold under ½" (1.3 cm) at ends of gimp, and butt folded ends together. Omit step 15 if decorative nails are not being used.

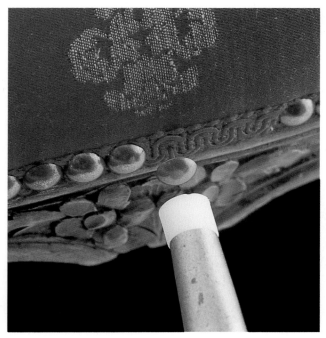

15) Tap the decorative nails into the wood, using upholstery hammer; center nails over gimp. Check the position of each nail before driving it in; if necessary, adjust vertical or horizontal position by tapping side of nail head slightly. Insert the nails head-to-head all around footstool.

16) Cut cambric 2" (5 cm) larger than the bottom of footstool. Fold under the edges of cambric; staple to the bottom of the footstool at 1" (2.5 cm) intervals.

Side chair has a decorative frame around the inset chair back and at the lower edge of the boxed seat. Double welting trims the seat, back, and arm posts.

Side Chairs

Small side chairs, often referred to as pull-up chairs, provide convenient extra seating when entertaining guests. The easy boxed-seat upholstery techniques on pages 84 to 89 can be used for a variety of side chair styles. These chairs may originally have padded boxed seats and inset backs, often framed with exposed decorative wood. Similar chairs may have pullover-style seats or loose boxed cushions. Chairs that originally had spring foundation seats can also be reupholstered using this easier method, if desired.

Before reupholstering, strip all layers of old fabric, padding, and burlap, and remove old webbing and any springs from the seat. Back webbing that is still in good condition and taut need not be replaced, unless the chair style has exposed wood with only a front tacking rail. Webbing must then be removed in order to replace the fabric that faces the back side of the chair. Refurbish the wood frame, if necessary.

✂ Cutting Directions

For the seat of the chair, cut a piece of burlap 3" (7.5 cm) larger than the chair frame. Cut cambric 2" (5 cm) larger than the bottom of the chair. Cut the fabric and the foam for the seat top as on page 84, step 2.

Cut the length of the boxing strip equal to the distance around the chair frame plus 2" (5 cm) overlap; if it is necessary to seam the boxing strip, add extra for seam allowances. For a chair with an exposed decorative seat frame, cut the width of the boxing strip equal to the foam thickness plus the distance from the top of the frame to the decorative wood plus 1½" (3.8 cm). For a chair without a decorative seat frame, cut the width of the boxing strip equal to the foam thickness plus the height of the frame plus 1½" (3.8 cm); the boxing strip wraps around to the bottom of the frame.

For the welting in the boxing seam, cut bias fabric strips, 1½" (3.8 cm) wide; the combined length of the strips is equal to the distance around the chair frame plus extra for seam allowances. For a chair with a decorative seat frame, also cut bias fabric strips, 3" (7.5 cm) wide, if double welting is to be used for the trim around the seat frame.

For the chair back, cut one rectangle of burlap, 5" (12.5 cm) larger than the frame opening. Cut two rectangles of fabric, 5" (12.5 cm) larger than

Side chair (above) is upholstered with a boxed seat that wraps under the chair frame. The inset chair back is trimmed with double welting.

the frame opening; these are to be used for the outside back and inside back pieces. Cut two or three layers of batting to the same size as the opening. If double welting is to be used, cut bias fabric strips, 3" (7.5 cm) wide.

For the chair arms, cut one rectangle of fabric, 4" (10 cm) larger than the area to be padded on the arm. Cut the batting to the size of the area to be padded. If double welting is to be used, cut bias fabric strips, 3" (7.5 cm) wide.

YOU WILL NEED

Decorator fabric; 2 yd. (1.85 m) is sufficient for most side chairs.

Welt cording, 5/32" (3.8 mm) diameter, for single welting and optional double welting.

Braid trim, such as gimp, if desired.

2 yd. (1.85 m) polyester or cotton upholstery batting, 27" (68.5 cm) wide.

Webbing and webbing stretcher.

Burlap, for reinforcing the seat and back.

1 yd. (0.95 m) cambric, for dustcover on bottom of chair.

Foam in 3" or 4" (7.5 or 10 cm) thickness, depending on style of chair; foam adhesive.

Hot glue gun and glue sticks, or white craft glue.

Staple gun; 3/8" or 1/2" (1 or 1.3 cm) staples.

How to Prepare the Chair and Sew the Boxed Seat

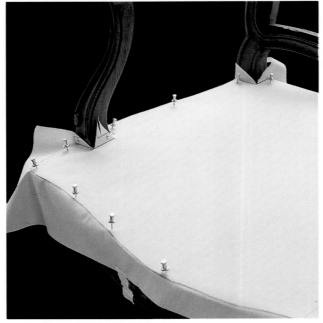

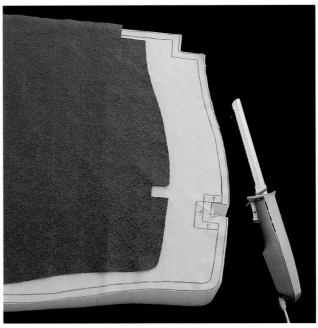

1) Make muslin pattern by placing muslin on frame, securing it with push pins. Mark muslin at edges of frame; draw around chair arms. For arms that slope out or back, redraw line ½" (1.3 cm) from original line so top of foam will fit around arm.

2) Remove muslin; add ½" (1.3 cm) seam allowances on all sides. Cut the fabric for seat top, following the pattern; cut the foam to same size for a firm, tight fit. Apply webbing (page 28) to chair frame; apply burlap as on page 78, step 2. Affix foam over burlap, using spray adhesive.

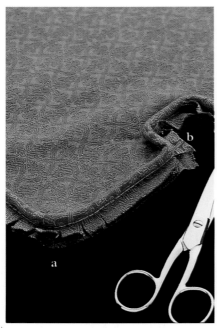

3) Make welting and attach to right side of seat top, as on page 46, steps 1 to 6. Clip seam allowances of the welting at ½" (1.3 cm) intervals on rounded corner **(a)** or make one diagonal clip at square corner **(b)**.

4) Fold back 1" (2.5 cm) at end of boxing strip; place strip on seat top, right sides together, with fold at center back. Stitch seam, crowding the cording; clip the corners as in step 3. At end of seam, overlap ends of boxing strip.

5) Cover the top and sides of foam with upholstery batting, cutting the batting around the arm posts; trim away excess batting at corners. For chair with a decorative seat frame, trim batting above decorative wood.

How to Upholster the Seat of a Chair with Side Arm Posts

Chair with decorative frame. 1) Place seat cover over the batting; staple-baste the boxing strip to the frame at center front, just above the decorative wood. Repeat at the center back.

2) Smooth top of seat cover from side to side; fold back the boxing strip at arm post. Mark a line for a Y-cut (page 69) from raw edge of boxing strip to within 2" (5 cm) of seam, aligning mark to center of arm post; cut on marked line.

3) Pull fabric down around the arm post. Repeat for opposite arm post.

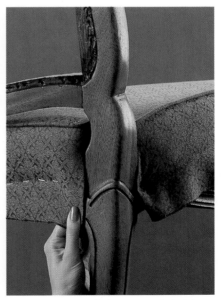

4) Remove staple at center back. At back corner, fold back boxing strip diagonally, as for chair with front arm posts on page 87, step 1. Mark line from raw edge to within 2" (5 cm) of seam, aligning mark to center of back post; cut on marked line. Repeat at opposite back post. Pull boxing strip down at back and side of chair frame.

5) Fold under fabric at side of chair, with fold along back post; staple boxing strip to chair frame at fold.

6) Repeat step 5 for opposite side of chair. On back of chair, staple boxing strip to frame, working from center toward sides. At back posts, fold under and staple fabric as in step 5.

(Continued on next page)

7) Pull fabric taut toward front of chair; staple boxing strip to front of frame, working from center toward sides of chair.

8) Fold under fabric along the front of the arm post as in step 5; staple boxing strip in front of arm post to frame.

9) Fold under fabric on the side of chair along back of arm post; staple boxing strip to side of the frame. Repeat for opposite side of chair.

10) Trim excess fabric on all sides of chair, just above decorative wood. Glue double welting (page 49) or gimp above the decorative wood, using hot glue or craft glue, making sure that raw edges and staples are covered. Butt the raw edges of double welting; or remove cording at ends and fold under edges. For gimp, fold under ends.

11) Fold under the edges of cambric; staple to the bottom of the chair at 1" (2.5 cm) intervals.

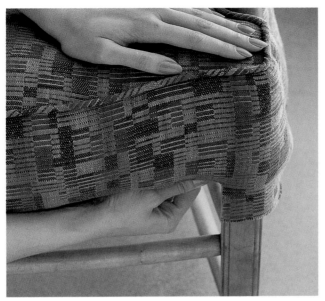

Chair without decorative frame. 1) Follow steps 1 to 7 on pages 84 to 86, except pull lower edge of boxing strip under frame, and staple to bottom of frame. Cut fabric at the front leg, from lower edge up to point where the leg and the bottom of frame meet; finish stapling boxing strip on front of chair frame up to the leg.

2) Cut fabric at side of chair, from lower edge up to point where leg and bottom of frame meet. At corner, trim excess fabric, allowing ¾" (2 cm) to fold under. Fold under fabric at front leg. Complete boxed seat as in steps 8 and 9, stapling lower edge to bottom of frame. Apply cambric as in step 11.

How to Upholster the Seat of a Chair with Front Arm Posts

Chair with decorative frame.
1) Follow step 1 on page 85. Smooth the top of the seat cover from side to side; align welting seams around the front arm posts. Fold back the boxing strip diagonally at the arm post. Mark a line from raw edge to within 2" (5 cm) of seam, aligning mark to center of arm post; cut on marked line.

2) Pull the fabric down around the arm post. Repeat for opposite arm post. Follow steps 4 to 7 on pages 85 and 86. On front of chair, fold under and staple the fabric at the arm post as in step 5. Complete seat as in steps 9 to 11, opposite.

Chair without decorative frame.
Follow steps 1 and 2, left, except pull lower edge of boxing strip around to bottom of chair frame, and staple to bottom of frame.

How to Upholster the Chair Back

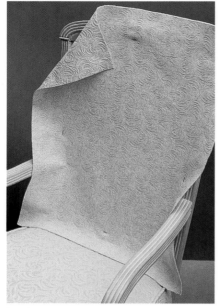

Tacking rail on inside back. 1) Apply fabric rectangle for outside back, with right side toward back of chair, staple-basting fabric at the center top to tacking rail on inside back of frame, ¼" (6 mm) from molding. Repeat at center bottom and center of each side.

2) Staple the fabric from the center bottom, up to the beginning of curve at rounded corners or up to 3" (7.5 cm) from square corners. Staple fabric at top, stretching fabric taut; repeat at each side. Staple fabric at the corners. Trim excess fabric next to staples. Place one layer of batting over fabric.

3) Apply the webbing strips as on page 31, stapling into tacking rail; webbing strips do not have to be folded over. Staple burlap over the webbing; trim excess.

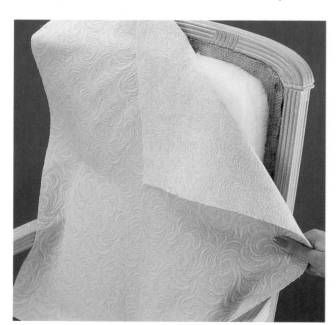

4) Place two layers of batting over the burlap. Place fabric rectangle for inside back, right side up, over batting; staple. Trim the excess fabric, and apply double welting or gimp as on page 86, step 10; butt ends of double welting, or fold under ends of gimp.

Tacking rails on inside and outside back. Follow steps 3 and 4, above and left. From back of chair, apply fabric rectangle for outside back, right side out, stapling into tacking rail on outside back of frame. Trim excess fabric, and apply double welting or gimp as on page 86, step 10.

How to Upholster the Chair Arms

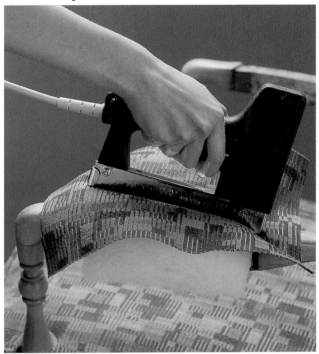

Wrapped arm pad. 1) Place two or three layers of batting on top of arm. Place fabric right side up over the batting; staple at back of arm.

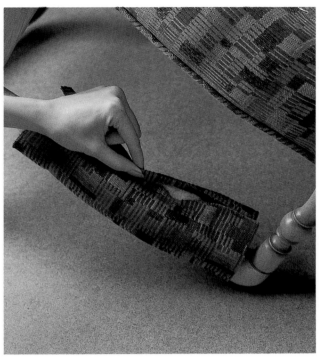

2) Stretch to front of arm; staple. Pull fabric around arm; staple to bottom of arm. On opposite side, pull fabric around arm, folding under edge; staple.

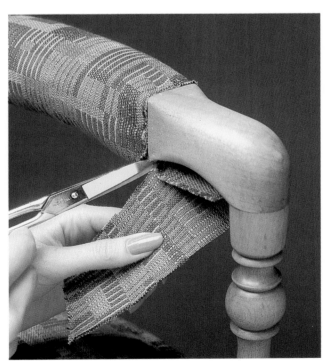

3) Finish stapling along back and front of arm. Trim excess fabric. Glue double welting or gimp as on page 86, step 10.

Oval arm pad. Place two or three layers of batting on top of arm. Place fabric right side up over the batting. Secure fabric as for chair back, steps 1 and 2, opposite. Trim excess fabric, and apply double welting or gimp as on page 86, step 10; butt ends of double welting, or fold under ends of gimp.

Skirted ottoman with attached box cushion matches the wing chair in design and pattern placement. The skirt style was changed in reupholstery to give the furniture an updated look.

Attached-cushion Ottomans

An ottoman is a popular furniture piece for living rooms and family rooms. This particular style is designed with a separate cushion which appears to be free but is actually attached to the ottoman base by a hidden seam. The cushion may be designed as a boxed cushion with or without welting, or as a welted knife-edge cushion.

The design features of the ottoman, often patterned after a matching chair, can vary in several ways. There may be a skirt (page 63), or it may have decorative legs. On some unskirted ottomans, the nosing, or base sides, are padded and there may be a welted band added around the lower edge.

Much of the outer cover is sewn together before it is attached to the ottoman. Take careful measurements of all the pieces before stripping, as accuracy will be crucial in constructing the new outer cover. As always, take careful notes when stripping the ottoman, and adjust the upholstery steps when necessary.

✂ Cutting Directions

Measure the ottoman (page 20), and record the measurements. Graph the fabric layout (page 22), according to the measurements and the allowances listed below. Mark the right side of the fabric, using chalk and following the graphed layout; label each piece. Cut out the pieces. Cut cambric 2" (5 cm) larger than the bottom of the ottoman.

For an ottoman with a boxed cushion, follow the cutting directions on page 50 for a boxed cushion that

Ottoman with welted band was reupholstered with a knife-edge cushion and given contemporary wooden bun feet.

will be sewn closed. For an ottoman with a knife-edge cushion, follow the cutting directions on page 58 for a cushion that will be exposed on all four sides.

Cut a piece for each side and end panel of the nosing 1" (2.5 cm) wider than the measured width before stripping. For a skirted ottoman, the cut length of each nosing piece is 5½" (14 cm) longer than the height of the ottoman from the lower edge to the upper edge. For an ottoman with a lower band, the cut length of each nosing piece is 5½" (14 cm) longer than the distance from the top of the band to the upper edge.

If the ottoman has a skirt, follow the cutting directions on page 63 for the desired skirt style.

If the ottoman has a lower band, cut pieces for the band 2½" (6.5 cm) longer and 1" (2.5 cm) wider than the measurements of the band pieces before stripping.

Cut fabric strips for the welting (page 45), with the total length equal to the total length of the welting, measured before stripping, plus additional length for seaming strips, joining ends, and inconspicuously positioning seams.

YOU WILL NEED

Graph paper.

Upholstery fabric; amount determined by measuring ottoman and graphing fabric layout.

Polyester batting or cotton batting.

Foam in desired density and thickness, polyester batting, for replacing cushion insert, if necessary.

Cambric, for dustcover on bottom of ottoman.

3" (7.5 cm) curved needle; heavy thread.

Staple gun and ⅜" (1 cm) staples.

Tack strip.

How to Upholster an Attached-cushion Ottoman

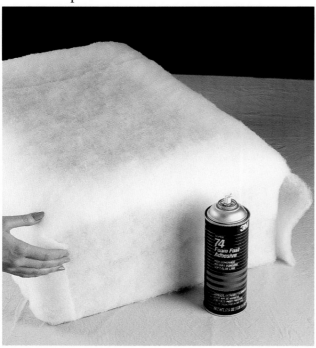

1) Strip ottoman (page 25); check foundation for stability. Make any necessary frame repairs (page 26); replace webbing (page 28) and retie springs (page 32), if necessary. Replace or supplement ottoman padding as necessary.

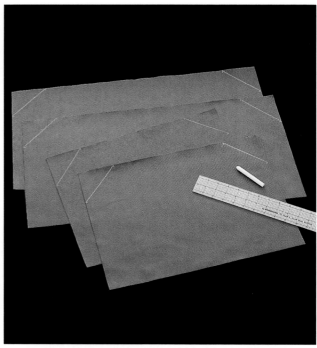

2) Mark points 3½" (9 cm) from top corners on sides and upper edges of nosing pieces. Draw seamlines on wrong side of nosing pieces, connecting marked points.

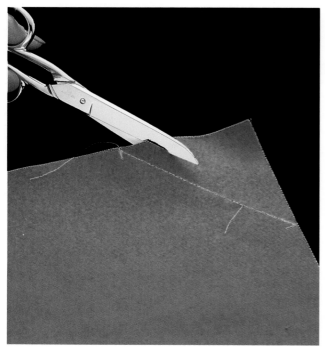

3) Pin nosing pieces, right sides together, forming continuous circle; stitch along marked lines, stopping 1½" (3.8 cm) from side edges. Trim seam allowances to ½" (1.3 cm); press open.

4) Mark lines at 45° angles from corners, on right side of cushion bottom, using chalk and straightedge. Place the nosing over cushion bottom, right sides together, aligning seams to marked diagonal lines; pin. Stitch ½" (1.3 cm) from inner edges of nosing.

5) Stitch ½" (1.3 cm) side seams of nosing, overlapping angled stitching lines at upper edges; round corners slightly. Trim as necessary. Press seams open.

6) Complete cushion cover as on page 55, steps 1 to 4 for boxed cushion or page 59, steps 1 and 2 for knife-edge cushion; tuck nosing inside cushion cover to keep free of stitches. Turn right side out.

7) Smooth cover in place over ottoman. Check fit; check for symmetry. Add padding, if necessary. Remove cover and adjust seams, if necessary.

8) Prepare and insert cushion as on pages 59 to 61.

(Continued on next page)

How to Upholster an Attached-cushion Ottoman (continued)

9) Flip nosing up, inside out, over cushion; place on ottoman base.

10) Pull nosing down over corners, one at a time, holding padding in place. Corner seams should fit snugly over base corners.

11) Pull nosing down taut over base; wrap to underside, and staple or tack securely at centers of sides. Then staple or tack nosing securely to underside of base, working from centers toward sides.

12) Fold under the edges of dustcover; staple to the bottom of the ottoman at 1" (2.5 cm) intervals. Make and attach skirt (page 63), if desired.

How to Upholster an Ottoman with a Welted Band

1) Follow steps 1 to 8 on pages 92 and 93. Pull the nosing down snugly over base; staple-baste near the lower edge. Staple securely just below placement line for lower band, stapling first at centers of sides and then working toward corners.

2) Stitch band pieces together into continuous circle, stitching ½" (1.3 cm) seams. Prepare welting as on page 64, steps 5 to 7. Sew welting to upper edge of band strip, matching pin marks to seams and easing band to fit.

3) Mark base with chalk at desired height of welt seam, measuring up from floor. Staple band to ottoman base as for skirt on page 65, steps 11 and 12.

4) Turn band down, pulling snugly over base; wrap to underside, and staple or tack securely at centers of sides. Then staple or tack band securely to underside of base, working from centers toward sides.

5) Staple welting to lower edge, if desired, following tips on page 48; place welting seam even with edge of base. Attach dustcover as in step 12, opposite.

Overstuffed Chairs

The upholstery techniques used for an overstuffed chair are commonly used for many other pieces of furniture. The term *overstuffed* simply means that the chair frame is completely covered with padding and fabric. The instructions that follow are a general guide for upholstering overstuffed chairs. Because styles and design details vary greatly, it is also necessary to refer to the notes, sketches, and photos taken while stripping your particular chair.

This chair is a simple style with an edge wire coil spring seat under a square cushion. Originally the chair had a boxed cushion; however, a new waterfall cushion was made, echoing the rounded curves of the back and arms.

Because there was extensive deterioration to the webbing and spring system, it was necessary to strip the chair to the frame in the seat area. The padding in the arms and back, however, was in good shape, so the remaining upholstery cover was loosened but left intact while working on the seat.

Begin the project by measuring all the chair parts and recording their measurements. Then determine the cut sizes of all the parts, and diagram the fabric layout (page 22). Strip the chair (page 25) as far as necessary. Loosen the lower edges of the inside arms and inside back, and staple-baste the lower edges to the rails to hold them in place. Check the frame for sturdiness and make any necessary repairs (page 26).

Below is a list of the materials that may be needed to reupholster a chair of this type. Depending on the condition of the chair, some existing materials, such as webbing or cushion foam, may be reused.

YOU WILL NEED

Upholstery fabric; amount determined after diagraming fabric layout.

Welt cording; amount determined after measuring chair.

Cotton batting.

Webbing.

Spring twine; button twine; #18 nylon thread.

Burlap.

Edge roll; same size originally used in chair.

Coirtex, for deck padding.

Denim, for deck cover.

High-resiliency foam in desired thickness, polyester batting, foam adhesive, for making a new cushion insert.

Lining fabric, such as lightweight, inexpensive upholstery fabric.

Cambric, for dustcover.

Cardboard tack strip.

Staple gun; ⅜" (1 cm) and ½" (1.3 cm) staples.

How to Upholster the Seat Area

1) Cut new edge roll, or use original; position edge roll, with flange turned toward back of chair and roll extending ¼" (6 mm) over burlap-covered edge wire. Thread 6" (15 cm) curved needle with button twine, cut twice the length of the edge roll.

2) Insert needle through front of edge roll and burlap at corner, hooking edge wire and leaving tail for knotting. Secure stitch with slipknot (page 34). Tie overhand knot (page 35) over slipknot. Stitch edge roll to burlap-covered edge wire, forming lock stitches 1" (2.5 cm) apart. Secure twine at end of edge roll with two overhand knots.

3) Stitch flange of edge roll to burlap, using same knots and stitches used on front of edge roll. Run twine under burlap between stitches. Mark nosing seamline on burlap 4" to 5" (10 to 12.5 cm) back from front edge of edge roll; mark center of line.

4) Mark center top and bottom of nosing fabric. Pin nosing fabric to chair along marked line, matching centers and extending fabric ½" (1.3 cm) over the marked line. Fold back nosing at outer edges; mark even with end of edge roll. Mark again even with crest of edge roll. (White tape was used for visibility.)

5) Remove nosing fabric. Draw line parallel to side from crest mark to upper edge **(a).** Measure line; mark point on side edge distance from top equal to length of first line **(b).** Mark another point ½" (1.3 cm) below first mark. Draw line from crest mark to second point **(c).** Cut out section, allowing ½" (1.3 cm) seam allowance. Repeat for opposite side.

6) Stitch ½" (1.3 cm) seam at corner, curving stitching line at fold. Repeat for opposite corner. Backstitch to secure. Press seam allowances toward center. Check fit.

7) Cut denim for deck, allowing ½" (1.3 cm) for nosing seam and 1½" (3.8 cm) beyond back and side rails for pulling and stapling. Mark center front and back. Align deck to nosing, matching center marks; pin. Stitch ½" (1.3 cm) seam, beginning and ending with backstitch 1½" (3.8 cm) beyond nosing seams.

8) Cut coirtex to fit seat, from ½" (1.3 cm) behind nosing seamline, extending 2" (5 cm) under arm rails and back rail; taper sides as necessary. Stitch coirtex to springs with button twine and curved needle, taking three to five stitches through burlap; secure stitches with overhand knots. Cover coirtex with one layer of cotton batting. Tear edges of batting; smooth into crevices under arms and back.

(Continued on next page)

9) Lay deck and nosing over seat. Fold nosing back, aligning seamline to marked line on burlap and matching centers; pin on each side of center. Pull seam allowance taut under arm; staple to top of side rail. Repeat for opposite side.

10) Thread 6" (15 cm) curved needle with button twine. Insert needle through seam allowance and burlap, hooking under edge wire and exiting on side of chair. Staple end of twine to top of side rail; pull twine in opposite direction, and staple again to secure.

11) Rethread needle on opposite end of twine. Stitch seam allowance to burlap, taking 1" (2.5 cm) running stitches near seamline; hook springs in stitches whenever possible. Secure end as in step 10.

12) Pull the deck under the back. Insert extra cotton between the coirtex and burlap to fill in depressions. Pull deck to back rail, matching centers; staple to top of rail. Continue stapling deck to back rail for several inches (centimeters) on each side of center.

13) Cut strip of coirtex ½" (1.3 cm) narrower than space between nosing seamline and edge roll. Stitch to burlap, as in step 8. Cover with two layers of cotton batting, torn to same size. Tear layer of cotton batting to fit from nosing seam to location of upper band attachment; smooth in place over other batting and edge roll. Tuck into crevices about 1" (2.5 cm).

14) Pull the nosing straight out and then down, matching center of nosing to center of front rail. Secure to face of rail, stapling several times near center. Fabric should be pulled snug, but not compress front of spring system. Smooth nosing down over padding across entire front. Staple to face of front rail as far as possible. Measure for consistent height from work surface.

15) Mark cutting line for fitting around arm post as shown; depth of Y-cut (page 69) should equal thickness of arm post. Cut on marked lines.

16) Pull nosing down toward side. Add padding as necessary. Staple cut edge to face of rail at base of arm post **(a).** Finish stapling nosing bottom to face of front rail. Push side nosing under arm to side of chair. Pull taut; staple to top of side rail **(b).**

(Continued on next page)

How to Upholster the Seat Area (continued)

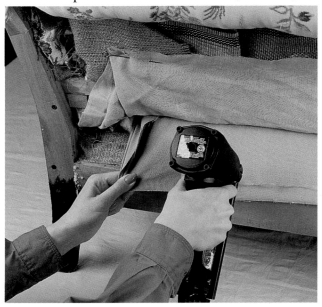

17) Add padding as needed between coirtex and burlap, along sides of deck. Pull deck fabric straight out under arm, and then downward toward back. Fabric should be taut but not compress springs. Staple deck sides to top of side rails to within 5" (12.5 cm) of back leg post.

18) Cut diagonally into back corner of deck, allowing fabric to straddle the back post (page 69); repeat for opposite corner. Push deck corner under back and arm; pull taut on either side of the back post. Turn under cut edges; staple to top of rails. Trim excess deck fabric even with top edge of rails.

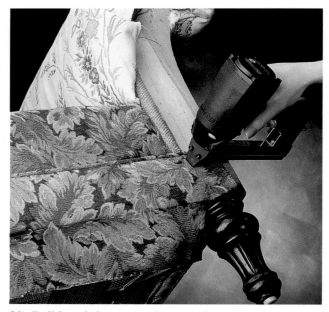

19) Stitch welting to top of band; turn seam allowance toward band. Place band on front rail; flip band up over welting. Place ½" (1.3 cm) tack strip over seam allowance, with upper edge of strip just under seamline. Staple through tack strip, securing upper edge of band; begin at center and work toward ends. Place layer of cotton batting over front rail, extending batting 1" (2.5 cm) above tack strip.

20) Pull band down; staple to underside of front rail, beginning at center. Batting forms double layer over tack strip. Clip fabric to lower edge of front rail at leg. Fold under fabric even with lower edge; staple ends to face of arm posts.

How to Upholster Inside Arms

1) Remove cover fabric from inside arm. Check the condition of padding, foundation fabric, and webbing. If webbing or foundation fabric must be replaced, carefully remove padding, keeping original shape intact. Replace necessary parts; replace padding. Remove any soiled batting; replace with new batting. Add new layer of batting as necessary.

2) Lay fabric over inside arm, aligning grainline. Check to see that ample fabric extends to front and back of arm. Measure chair from outer corner of nosing to base of arm post **(a).** Smooth fabric into crease at outer edge of deck. Measure same distance from crease toward lower edge; mark. Draw cutting line from mark to lower edge; draw Y-cut with width same as width of arm post. Cut on marked line.

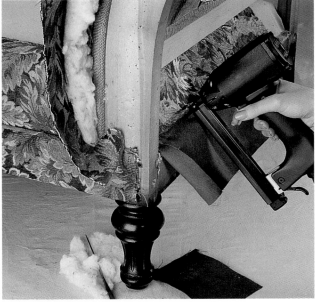

3) Separate fabric at cut; pull fabric down, straddling arm post. Staple to front arm post and behind arm post on top of side rail. Pull bottom edge of arm fabric over side rail; staple to top of rail to within 8" (20.5 cm) of back rail. Pull top edge of arm fabric over top of arm. Staple once at center of outer surface of arm rail.

4) Measure from point where inside arm meets back to arm stretcher post or back post just below top arm rail. Mark point this distance from back edge on the horizontal grain of fabric. Measure again just above arm stretcher rail; mark. Draw cutting line from each point to back edge; depth of Y-cuts should equal thickness of arm stretcher post or back post. Cut on marked lines.

(Continued on next page)

5) Pull fabric through to the outside; staple section between cuts to arm stretcher post, if any. If there is not an arm stretcher post, as in this chair, pin fabric temporarily to arm webbing. Section will be permanently attached to side of back leg post after inside back is attached.

6) Cut lower corner diagonally to point where it must straddle back leg post. Pull section above diagonal cut **(a)** to inside of back leg post; fold under cut edge, and staple. Trim excess. Leave open at back of side rail **(b).** Section will be finished after the inside back is attached.

7) Make short relief cut (page 69) off original cut at upper back curve of arm; make additional cuts as necessary to mold fabric over curve, making each cut off the one that preceeds it. Trim fabric as necessary. Turn under flaps of fabric; pull fabric snugly into crevice. Staple near top back corner of arm rail.

8) Staple back of inside arm to side of back post, clipping and forming pleats as necessary. Finish stapling fabric to outer surface of arm rail from center to back.

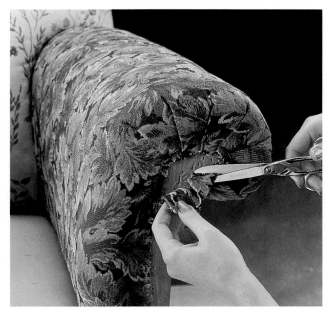

9) Pull front inside arm down, forming fold over the nosing; staple. Pull fabric taut across arm front, and staple, keeping grain parallel to lower edge and working upward to point of first pleat. Trim fabric up to top staple. Form pleat, using flat end of regulator; staple over fold. Trim excess fabric. Repeat around entire curve, spacing pleats evenly.

10) Finish stapling underside of wrapped arm to the outer surface of arm rail; clip to the rail as necessary. Check for tight, smooth fit. Release staples in top of side rail; restretch and restaple fabric. Repeat steps 1 to 10 for opposite arm.

How to Upholster Inside Back

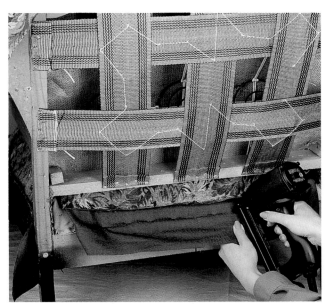

1) Remove all staples and tacks holding inside back. If foundation needs repair, remove padding with the cover to keep padding intact. Retie springs and apply new burlap, if necessary. Replace cover and padding; remove cover. Replace or supplement padding as necessary. Place fabric over inside back; align center marks. Staple-baste at center on back of top rail.

2) Push fabric through crevice between back and deck. Pull taut; staple at center of back rail. Continue to pull and staple fabric for several inches (centimeters) on each side of center. Pull and staple upper edge, working outward from center, until fabric cannot be controlled without pleats.

(Continued on next page)

How to Upholster Inside Back (continued)

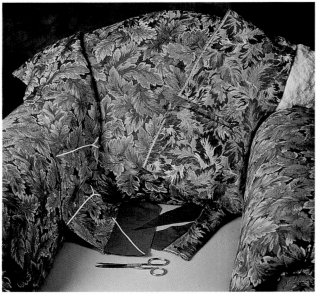

3) Measure distance from each back deck corner to back leg posts. Mark these points on inside back fabric. Mark for diagonal cuts from corners of fabric; cut. Measure distance from intersection of back and inside arm to back post at top arm rail and again at arm stretcher rail, on each side. Mark these points on inside back fabric. Mark for Y-cut horizontally from outer edges of fabric to each point. Cut.

4) Pull fabric section through space between top arm rail and arm stretcher rail. Pull taut; staple to inner surface of back leg post **(a).** Separate fabric at diagonal cut, allowing fabric to straddle back leg post. Pull fabric taut and finish stapling to top of back rail **(b)** and top of side rail **(c).** Finish stapling lower back edge of inside arm to top of side rail **(d),** where it was left open from step 6 on page 104. Trim excess fabric.

5) Make short relief cut (page 69) off upper Y-cut where inside back wraps over arm; make additional relief cuts as necessary to mold fabric over curve, making each cut off the one that preceeds it. Trim fabric as necessary; turn under flaps of fabric. Pull fabric snugly into crevice and toward back of chair. Staple to back of back leg post, working upward until fabric cannot be controlled without pleats.

6) Pleat out fullness on upper corner, as on page 105, step 9. Work upward from side to top. Repeat for opposite side, turning pleats in opposite direction and spacing pleats to match first side. Trim excess fabric at upper and side edges.

7) Remove pins holding the inside arm flap **(a)** to webbing. Pull fabric taut, and staple to inner surface of back leg post, over inside back fabric **(b)**.

8) Check arm and back padding around deck and along inside back edges, making sure that both sides are padded equally and without gaps. Add padding as necessary, inserting padding from back and sides of chair. Make any final adjustments necessary in tautness of outer fabric. Remove pins holding arm webbing; staple webbing to inner surface of back leg post. Trim excess fabric in areas that have not yet been trimmed. Make cushion (page 50).

How to Upholster Outside Arms and Outside Back

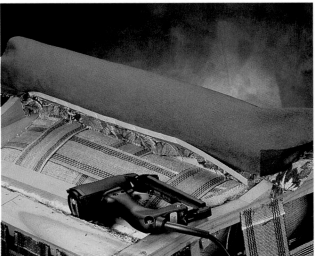

1) Place chair on its side. Mark line on underside of top arm rail in line with outer surfaces of front arm post and back post. Position outside arm fabric with horizontal grainline parallel to lower edge of chair; allow at least 1½" (3.8 cm) excess fabric to extend over front, back, and lower edges. Mark upper edge, even with line on rail; mark centers on rail and fabric. Trim upper edge ½" (1.3 cm) above marked line. Cut lining, using outside arm piece as pattern.

2) Place outside arm fabric, facedown, over roll of inside arm, aligning marked line on fabric to marked line on rail. Place lining over fabric, aligning edges; staple-baste within ½" (1.3 cm) allowance. Place cardboard tack strip over ½" (1.3 cm) allowance, aligning outer edge to marked line. Staple through tack strip and fabrics, stapling diagonally near outer edge of strip.

(Continued on next page)

3) Smooth lining down taut over outside arm. Staple to outer surface of side rail, front arm post, and back post. Trim just inside the outer edges. Place half layer cotton batting over outside arm, extending 1" (2.5 cm) beyond outer edge of tack strip. Tear even with frame edges on bottom, front, and back.

4) Pull outside arm fabric down taut over padding. Staple to underside of side rail at center; continue stapling to within about 4" (10 cm) of front and back legs.

5) Clip into fabric as necessary on curve of arm. Pull fabric taut, and staple to face of front arm post. Clip fabric to lower edge of side rail behind front leg. Fold under fabric even with lower edge of side rail; pull taut across front of leg. Staple to front arm post.

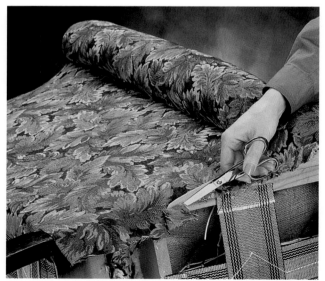

6) Pull upper edge of outside arm around back rail; staple. Clip fabric to lower edge of side rail in front of back leg. Fold under fabric even with lower edge of side rail; pull taut around back leg. Staple to back post. Finish stapling outside arm along back post and underside of side rail. Trim excess fabric.

7) Attach welting to outer edges of back, following straight lines and curves established by the chair frame. Attach cardboard tack strip, if outside back will be hand-sewn. Position outer edge of strip just shy of welting seamline. Staple diagonally in straight areas. Notch strip for turning corners; staple parallel to outer edge in notched areas. Attach lining piece, stapling inside inner edge of tack strip and even with lower edge of back rail; trim.

8) Place half layer cotton batting over outside back lining. Tear even with inner edge of tack strip and lower edge of bottom rail. Place outside back fabric over batting. Staple-baste to underside of back rail to within about 4" (10 cm) of back legs. Clip fabric to rail at inner edge of legs. For attaching outside back with flexible metal tacking strip, omit steps 9 to 12; follow page 119, steps 13 to 16, attaching continuous tacking strip around sides and top.

9) Trim upper edge near center to within ½" (1.3 cm) of outer edge of welt; turn under ½" (1.3 cm), and pin. Repeat at center sides. Then trim remaining edges to ½" (1.3 cm); turn under, and pin.

10) Blindstitch (page 69) outside back panel to welting, using 3" curved needle and #18 nylon thread. Knot end; take first few stitches into welt seamline in one upper corner, stitching away from center to lock stitches. Reverse direction; stitch across top and down one side, spacing stitches ½" (1.3 cm) apart.

(Continued on next page)

How to Upholster Outside Arms and Outside Back (continued)

11) Continue stitching to just above leg. Fold fabric under even with lower edge; stitch to lower edge. Run needle through to opposite side of welting, coming out at lower edge of outside arm. Run thread through fold over leg to front edge of leg.

12) Staple thread several times to underside of side rail, changing direction of thread with each staple. Repeat steps 10 and 11 for remaining side of outside back; secure thread. Remove basting staples from back rail; pull lower edge taut, and staple to underside of back rail.

How to Attach Cambric and Front Arm Panels

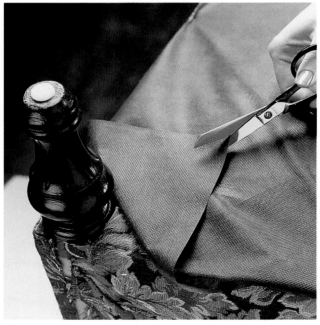

1) Cut cambric 3" (7.5 cm) larger than the measurements of bottom of chair between outer edges of rails. Fold under just shy of outer edge of rail; staple at center front, back, and sides. Fold cambric back at corner, so fold is even with inner corner of leg. Cut diagonally from corner of fabric to fold. Repeat for each corner.

2) Fold under cut edges, so folds are tight against sides of leg; staple in place. Finish stapling front, back, and sides, folding cambric under just shy of outer edge of rail.

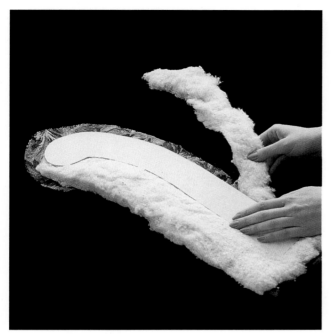

3) Cut fabric for arm panels 1½" (3.8 cm) larger on all sides than arm panel base. Place fabric facedown on work surface. Place batting over fabric; place arm panel base over batting. Tear batting even with edge of arm panel base.

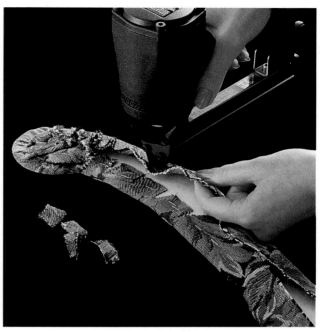

4) Pull fabric taut to back side of base, and staple at centers of sides and at top of curve. Clip fabric along inside curve; pull taut, and staple. Pull taut and staple around outer curve, easing in fullness. Pull taut and staple at the bottom edge. Pleat out excess fabric at bottom corners; staple.

5) Staple welting to outer edge, beginning and ending at bottom of sides. Follow tips on page 48. Outer edge of base should just cover welting seamline on front of arm panel.

6) Separate threads of weave to make hole for nail, using point of regulator (page 11). Insert #15 or #17 finishing nail; drive into arm. Insert additional nails as necessary. Close holes in weave after driving in nails. Inspect chair. Adjust padding as necessary, using regulator. Steam chair (page 68).

Lawson-style Chairs

A Lawson-style chair is identified by its boxed arms, boxed and buttoned back, and simple lines. The padding is minimal, cushioning the corners of the arms and back, but allowing the lines to remain rather sharp. Depending on the chair's age, the support in the deck and back may consist of sinuous springs (page 33) or, as with the deck and lower back of this chair, an enclosed manufactured coil spring system.

The nosing of this chair has a hard edge, cushioned by an edge roll that is attached directly to the front rail. The deck is then prepared in a manner similar to that for the overstuffed chair, but without the corner darts.

Much of the outer cover of a Lawson-style chair is sewn together before it is attached to the frame. On this particular chair, the top arms, front arms, and front band are cut as one piece and sewn with welted seams to the inside arms, outside arms, and nosing of the chair. The nosing is hand-sewn to the deck, and then the entire unit is placed over the lightly padded frame and secured. Because the fabric must slide over the batting in the fitting process, polyester batting is recommended.

The method for attaching buttons (pages 117 and 118, steps 7 to 9) allows for easy replacement of any damaged buttons. By depressing the inside back of the chair, the slackened twine can be looped back over the button face and released from the shank. The twine loop is then inserted into the shank of the new button and looped over the button face to secure it.

Begin the project by measuring all the chair parts and recording their measurements. Then determine the cut sizes of all the parts, and diagram the fabric layout (page 22). Strip the chair (page 25) as far as necessary. Loosen the lower edges of the inside arms and inside back, and staple-baste the lower edges to the rails to hold them in place. Check the frame for sturdiness, and make any necessary repairs (page 26). From the materials list below, select items that will be necessary for your project, depending on the condition of existing materials.

YOU WILL NEED

Upholstery fabric; amount determined after diagraming fabric layout.

Welt cording; amount determined after measuring chair.

Polyester batting.

Webbing.

Spring twine; button twine; #18 nylon thread.

Burlap.

Edge roll; same size originally used in chair.

Coirtex, for deck padding.

Denim, for deck cover.

High-resiliency foam in desired thickness, polyester batting, foam adhesive, for making a new cushion insert.

Lining fabric, such as lightweight, inexpensive upholstery fabric.

Cambric, for dustcover.

Cardboard tack strip.

Flexible metal tacking strip.

Staple gun; ⅜" (1 cm) and ½" (1.3 cm) staples.

How to Upholster the Deck and Arms

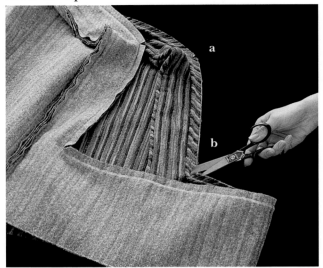

1) Stitch welting to front and top edges of outside arm panel. Stitch boxing to front and top of outside arm, aligning lower edge of front boxing to lower edge of outside arm. Repeat for opposite arm. Stitch welting to remaining edge of boxing and front band. Mark seam allowances of boxing directly across from top front corners of outside arms (**a**). Clip seam allowances at upper corners of band (**b**).

2) Stitch inside arm to boxing, aligning mark on boxing to top front corner of inside arm. Backstitch at clip. Repeat for opposite arm. Center nosing on front band. Stitch nosing to front band between clips, backstitching at clips. Stitch deck to nosing, matching centers. Mark placement line for nosing seam on spring cover; mark center. Mark center of nosing seam allowance. Attach deck as on page 100, steps 9 to 13, omitting references to edge wire and covering nosing with one layer of batting. Add half layer of batting from nosing seam to lower edge of front rail.

3) Replace webbing on inside arm, if necessary. Cover inside arms with burlap. Attach burlap to outside arms, leaving unattached along lower edge and for short distance at lower front and back. Supplement or replace padding on arms as necessary. Turn arm cover inside out; position front boxing in place over arm front. Turn arm cover right side out; smooth in place over chair arm, turning welted seam allowances toward inside and outside arm panels. Repeat for remaining arm.

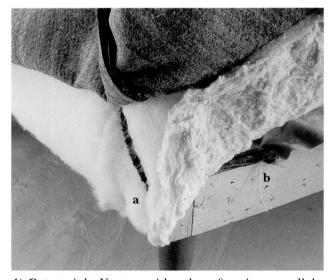

4) Cut straight Y-cut on side edge of nosing, parallel to front edge, allowing fabric to fit around front arm post; front point of Y-cut is aligned to nosing seamline. Pull nosing down to front and side, straddling front arm post with opposite sides of Y-cut (**a** and **b**). Pull taut; staple. Finish stapling nosing and deck to top of side rail. Repeat for opposite side.

5) Pull front band taut; staple to underside of front rail for several inches (centimeters) at center. Cut diagonally into lower front edge of inside arm, allowing fabric to fit around front arm post. Fold under cut edge of inside arm from corner of nosing to point of cut (**a**); pull lower edge of inside arm under arm stretcher rail.

6) Cut Y-cut in boxing at back top of arm, allowing fabric to fit around back post. Cut second Y-cut on back edge of inside arm, allowing the fabric to fit around back stretcher rail. Fold under edges of Y-cut on boxing. Pull inside arm through to back of chair. Pull taut; staple to inner side of back rail.

7) Pull lower edge of inside arm taut to side rail (**a**), pulling welting along upper arm slightly to inside (**b**). Staple lower edge of inside arm to top of the side rail.

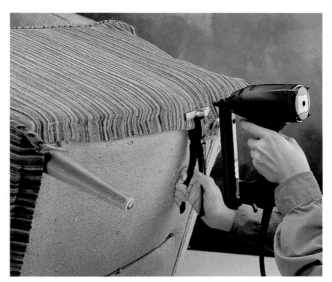

8) Pull outside arm taut, realigning welting along top of arm. Staple lower edge to underside of side rail, up to within several inches (centimeters) of back corner. Staple back edge to outside of back post, leaving unattached several inches (centimeters) from top and bottom. Finish stapling front band to underside of front rail.

How to Upholster the Inside and Outside Back

1) Place the rectangle of fabric for inside back over existing inside back, cutting shallow relief cuts (**a**) to fit around the arms; pin. Mark seamline around outer edge, using chalk. Cut out inside back ½" (1.3 cm) beyond marked seamline. Cut top back boxing to same width as upper cut edge of inside back, with length of boxing equal to finished length of existing boxing plus 2" (5 cm). Cut boxing for sides of back to same size as existing boxing, allowing ½" (1.3 cm) seam allowances on edges that adjoin inside back and 1½" (3.8 cm) pulling and stapling allowance on edge that gets pulled to back of chair.

2) Stitch welting to outer edge of inside back, avoiding any welting seams on top of back. Stitch top back boxing to side back boxing pieces, using ½" (1.3 cm) seams; press open. Pin boxing to inside back, right sides together, matching boxing seams to top corners. Stitch, using welting foot or zipper foot.

3) Remove existing back cover. Supplement or replace padding as necessary. Place back cover, inside out, over padding. Turn the cover right side out, fitting corners snugly; smooth in place over the chair back, turning welted seam allowances toward inside back. Pull taut; secure to outside of top back rail at center.

4) Cut horizontal Y-cuts in side boxing, allowing the fabric to fit around top arm rail and arm stretcher rail. Pull taut, pulling boxing above top cut to outside of back post (**a**) and boxing between cuts to inside of back post (**b**); staple over inside arm fabric (**c**).

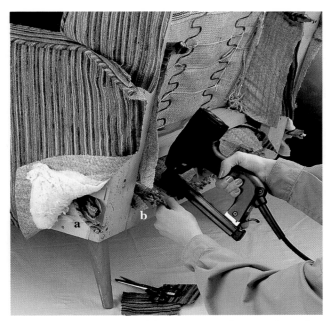

5) Cut boxing along welting seams at lower edge of inside back, allowing fabric to straddle back leg post. Pull welting taut; staple to top of the side rail **(a).** Pull remaining lower edge taut; staple to top of the back rail **(b).**

6) Finish pulling and stapling boxing to back of back posts and top rail. Pull top of outside arm taut over inside back; staple to back of back post. Finish stapling outside arms under side rails.

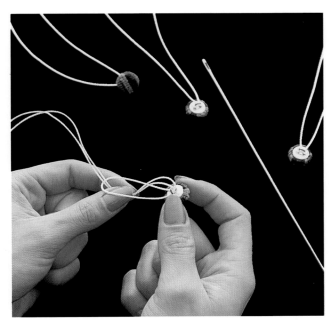

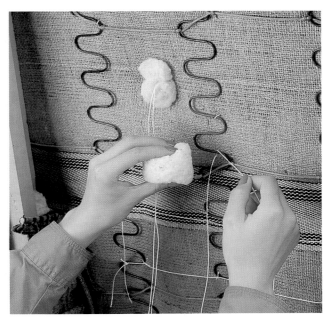

7) Pin-mark positions of buttons on inside back. Cut button twine about 25" (63.5 cm) long; fold in half. Insert fold of twine through shank eye of button; loop twine over button, so that twine wraps around shank, but moves freely. Insert cut ends of twine through eye of button needle.

8) Insert needle through chair back at one pin mark. Pull twine through until button shank enters fabric. Separate twines at back of chair, straddling a spring, if possible. Tie twines around wad of batting, using slipknot (page 34).

(Continued on next page)

9) Repeat step 8 for each button. Tighten all knots equally, checking indentations of buttons on inside back. Secure knots with overhand knots. Pull twines taut to top rail; staple securely. Make any final adjustments necessary in tautness of outer fabric. Trim excess fabric in areas that have not yet been trimmed. Make cushion (page 50).

10) Attach welting to outer edges of back sides and top, beginning and ending at bottom of back rail. Encase cording at ends as on page 48, step 1. Attach lining to back, trimming even with cut edge of welting. Place outside back fabric over outside back. Trim to size, allowing ½" (1.3 cm) excess along the top, 1" (2.5 cm) along the sides, and 1½" (3.8 cm) along the bottom.

11) Flip fabric up over back of chair. Align cut edge of fabric to cut edge of upper welting, matching centers. Place cardboard tack strip over ½" (1.3 cm) allowance, aligning outer edge to welting seamline. Staple across top.

12) Cut half layer of batting to fit between seamlines of welting at top and sides and even with bottom of back rail. Staple-baste at top and side centers.

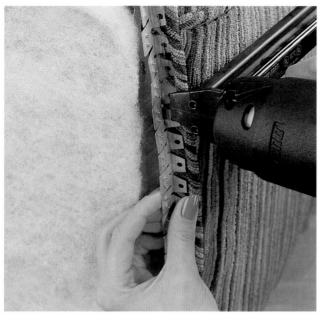

13) Staple metal tacking strip to sides, aligning outer edge of tacking strip to welting seamline. Begin at upper welting seamline; end at bottom of back rail, opening strip as necessary for ease in stapling. Position stapler so one leg of staple goes through each hole in tacking strip.

14) Close tacking strip to about 30°. Wrap batting over edge of strip to cushion sharp edge.

15) Pull down outside back fabric; staple-baste to bottom of back rail, matching centers. Trim fabric to ½" (1.3 cm) along sides. Tuck fabric into tacking strip opening, using regulator. Push tacking strip closed along both sides. Hammer tacking strip securely, using mallet or tack hammer.

16) Pull lower edge taut; staple to underside of back rail. Attach the welting to underside of rails around bottom of chair, joining ends as on page 48, steps 1 and 2. Attach cambric as on page 110, steps 1 and 2.

Wing Chairs

The upholstery steps required for a wing chair include techniques used in both the overstuffed chair and the Lawson-style chair. Wing chairs generally have curved pullover inside backs, upholstered in the same manner as the overstuffed chair. Close-fitting arms may be boxed and upholstered in a manner similar to the Lawson-style chair, or, as is the case with this chair, the inside arms and front arm panels are sewn together and attached to the chair; the outside arms are attached with metal tacking strips.

Wing chairs usually have a hard edge spring system, which may consist of sinuous springs or coil springs. An edge roll is attached directly to the top of the front rail. The nosing wraps around the front corners of the chair, and the seat holds a T-cushion. Welting defines the lower and outer edges of the wings, the top of the outside back, the front arm panels, and the lower edge of the chair.

Begin the project by measuring all the chair parts and recording their measurements. Then determine the cut sizes of all the parts and diagram the fabric layout (page 22). Strip the chair (page 25) as far as necessary. Loosen the lower edges of the inside arms and inside back, and staple-baste the lower edges to the rails to hold them in place. Check the frame for sturdiness, and make any necessary repairs (page 26).

From the materials list below, select items that will be necessary for your project, depending on the condition of existing materials.

YOU WILL NEED

Upholstery fabric; amount determined after diagraming fabric layout.

Welt cording; amount determined after measuring chair.

Polyester batting or cotton batting.

Burlap.

Edge roll; same size originally used in chair.

Coirtex, for deck padding.

Denim, for deck cover.

High-resiliency foam in desired thickness, polyester batting, foam adhesive, for making a new cushion insert.

Lining fabric, such as lightweight, inexpensive upholstery fabric.

Cambric, for dustcover.

Cardboard tack strip.

Flexible metal tacking strip.

Staple gun; ⅜" (1 cm) and ½" (1.3 cm) staples.

How to Upholster a Wing Chair

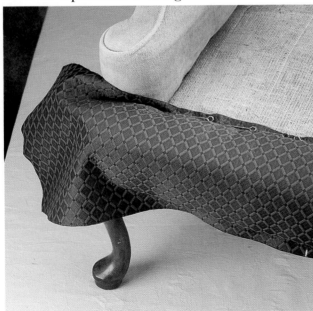

1) Mark nosing seamline on burlap 4" to 5" (10 to 12.5 cm) back from front edge of edge roll; mark center of line. Center nosing fabric faceup over chair nosing, with upper edge of fabric extending ½" (1.3 cm) beyond marked line. Pin along upper edge. Pull fabric down over padding; staple-baste to underside of front rail in several places.

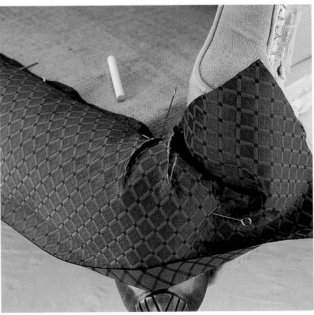

2) Fold out fabric at front corners to conform to the shape of the chair. Chalk-mark corner folds.

(Continued on next page)

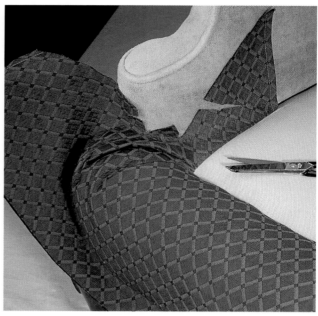

3) Remove fabric from the chair; check to see that marked folds match corresponding marks on opposite corner. Stitch folds as marked, backstitching at cut edges. Tie threads at points. Trim to ½" (1.3 cm). Smooth nosing in place over chair; check fit. Adjust, if necessary.

4) Stitch nosing to deck fabric, matching centers; pivot at corners of nosing. Attach deck as on pages 99 to 101, steps 8 to 13, omitting reference to edge wire in step 10. Pull nosing down; staple to underside of front rail at the center. Cut Y-cut on each side of nosing, allowing fabric to fit around front arm posts; cut relief cuts (page 69) as necessary.

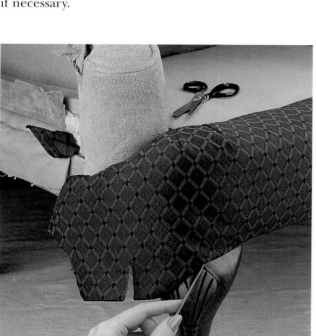

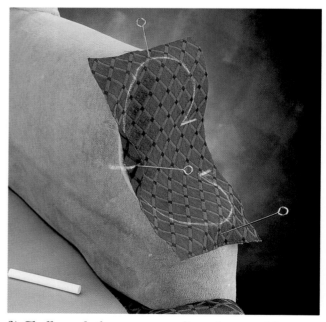

5) Clip lower edge of nosing just to bottom of rail in front of and behind decorative leg. Turn under nosing between clips, tucking fabric under padding. Pull taut; staple along fold, if necessary, but only if the lower edge will be finished with welting. Finish stapling nosing to front and side rails; finish deck as on page 102, steps 17 and 18.

6) Chalk-mark three or more lines for matching around existing front arm panel, placing two marks at beginning and end of welting seam. Place front arm panel fabric faceup over front arm panel; chalk-mark seamline. Transfer matching lines.

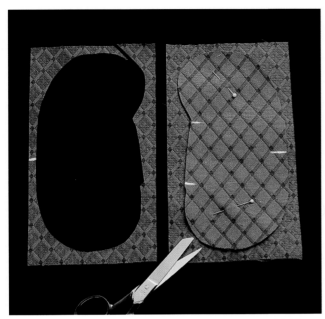

7) **Remove** fabric; cut out the front arm panel ½" (1.3 cm) beyond seamline. Cut mirror-image panel for opposite arm.

8) **Place** inside arm fabric over existing inside arm, wrapping around front arm post and over top arm rail; chalk-mark seamline around front arm panel. Transfer matching lines. Remove fabric. Cut out inside arm around front panel, ½" (1.3 cm) beyond seamline. Cut mirror image for opposite inside arm.

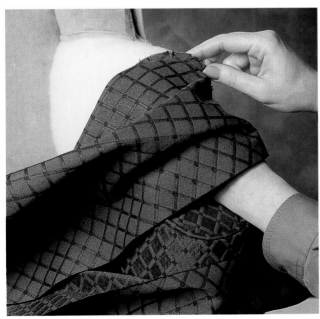

9) **Stitch** welting around front arm panel, following design of original cover. Pin inside arm to front arm panel, matching marked lines; stitch. Remove old arm cover. Supplement or replace arm padding as necessary. Place new arm cover, inside out, over arm, holding front arm panel in place.

10) **Smooth** arm cover back over arm. Pull taut. Cut Y-cuts and relief cuts (page 69) as necessary. Staple the lower edge of inside arm to top of side rail (**a**) to within several inches (centimeters) of the back post. Staple top side edge to top arm rail (**b**). Staple front side edge to outside of front arm post (**c**). Check to see that relief cuts and staples at top back of arm (**d**) will be hidden under wing welting.

(Continued on next page)

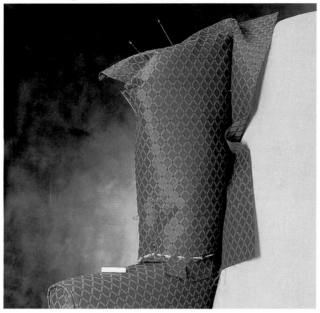

11) Place inside wing fabric faceup over existing inside wing, aligning grainlines; pin. Cut shallow relief cuts up to welting at lower edge. Chalk-mark lower welting seamline.

12) Remove fabric. Trim excess fabric ½" (1.3 cm) below marked seamline. Cut mirror-image piece for opposite inside wing. Mark location of welting on chair frame; remove old cover fabric from the inside wing.

13) Supplement or replace wing padding as necessary. Place inside wing over padding, aligning welting to marks on frame. Pull welting snug; staple.

14) Cut Y-cut near back upper edge of inside wing, allowing fabric to straddle top back rail. Pull fabric through crevice between wing and back; staple to inside of back post.

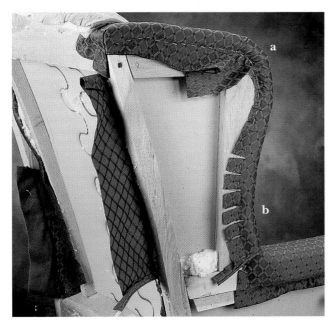

15) Smooth fabric over front wing post and top wing rail, wrapping to outside. Pull taut, and staple, working upward from welting. Pleat out fabric as necessary **(a)**; cut relief cuts at curves as necessary **(b)**. Trim excess fabric.

16) Upholster inside back as for overstuffed chair on pages 105 to 107, steps 1 to 8, omitting step 5. Attach welting in one continuous piece to outside curve of wings and across upper back. Flatten bulky areas with mallet.

17) Attach lining and batting to outside wing as on page 118, steps 10 and 12. Place outside wing fabric over batting, aligning grainline; staple-baste along outside back rail. Attach fabric to welted edge, using flexible metal tacking strip as on page 119, steps 13 to 15. Release basting staples at back; pull taut, and staple. Staple lower edge to outside of top arm rail.

18) Upholster outside arm, using cardboard tack strip along upper edge and flexible metal tacking strip along front edge. Upholster outside back and finish chair as on pages 118 and 119, steps 10 to 16; for curved upper back, use flexible metal tacking strip instead of cardboard. Trim seam allowance from welting where it wraps over decorative legs.

Index

Sources for product information:

A-1 Foam Specialities Co., Inc.
7608 Lyndale Avenue So.
Richfield, MN 55423
(612) 861-5255

Do-It-Yourself Upholstery Supply
1558 Larpenteur Avenue
St. Paul, MN 55113
(612) 645-7211

New York Fabrics, Inc.
800-328-2700

Rochford Supply, Inc.
800-334-6414

Creative Publishing international, Inc.
offers a variety of how-to books. For
information write:
    Creative Publishing international, Inc.
     Subscriber Books
    5900 Green Oak Drive
    Minnetonka, MN 55343